THE
STRENGTHS
OF
BLACK
FAMILIES

THE
STRENGTHS
OF
BLACK
FAMILIES

ROBERT B. HILL
Director
Research Department
National Urban League

EMERSON HALL PUBLISHERS, INC.
New York

First Edition

ISBN 0-87829-008-7

Library of Congress Catalog Card Number 70-188563

Ernest Crichlow, Jacket Art
Anita Duncan, Design
Joe Meachem, Jacket Typography
The Book Press, Composition, Printing and Binding

Distributed by
Independent Publishers' Group
60 E. 55th Street, New York, N.Y. 10022

In Memory of Whitney M. Young, Jr.

Executive Director
National Urban League
1961–1971

TABLE
OF
CONTENTS

PREFACE

One of the great American sports is called "blaming the victim." Anyone can play; all that's needed is a readily identifiable victim, a deep-rooted set of myths and stereotypes, and a rigid, determined refusal to face facts.

Perhaps the most popular variant of "blaming the victim" is to talk about "the weakness of black families." It's a game that has been played by many people, but the most avid players seem to be sociologists and urbanologists searching for a reason for black disadvantage in our society. The myths basic to the game are familiar to all: that the black family is "matriarchal," it is unstable, it does not prepare black people for productive lives, and it is the prime source of black economic weakness. These myths have moved from discredited folklore to the respectability of learned scholarly papers replete with charts, diagrams, and theoretical conceptualizations. Worse still, they have become acceptable to those who determine public policy, as well as those in the media who publicize those policies.

With the publication of *The Strengths of Black Families*, the National Urban League's Research Director, Dr. Robert Hill, has taken a giant step in stripping away the myths and stereotypes that have been the underpinning for this disastrous game. Using rigorous social science methodology, Dr. Hill's analysis discloses the weaknesses of previous biased studies, and uncovers a wealth of evidence that gives the lie to myths surrounding the black family.

Few people, after reading this book, will readily believe the myths of matriarchy, dependence, illegitimacy, or the related web of erroneous misinformation that has surrounded this subject. Readers will find, instead, what black people have known all along: that despite tremendous odds, the black family has been a bulwark of black achievement, that it has proved a flexible and adaptable instrument of black survival, and that it has been the nourishing foundation of positive aspects of the black experience.

With the publication of this study, I hope the malicious game of blaming the black family for the results of discrimination and oppression will be ended. The games people have played in this area have been destructive and cruel—other obstacles among the many blacks have had to survive. When our scholars, politicians, administrators and the general public stop playing this myth-bound game and come to understand that the disadvantage black Americans suffer is due solely to the malfunctioning of our economic system and the evil heritage of racism and discrimination, we shall be better able to build a society that is more just and equal. This important study is a vital step in that direction.

Vernon E. Jordan, Jr.
Executive Director
National Urban League

FOREWORD

In *Strengths of Black Families,* Robert Hill has amassed, analyzed and interpreted a wealth of data bearing on the manner in which Black families have been able to survive and indeed, move beyond survival to a high level of existence and humanity in a hostile environment. In this study, Dr. Hill has recaptured for the National Urban League a role in the analysis and interpretation of life within the Black community which was so nobly expressed in the pages of the magazine, *Opportunity,* which has long since been abandoned. At the same time, he has brought a renewed focus to some of the positive aspects of the Black experience. For this he will be criticized by many readers of this report, for how can one speak of Black families and strengths in the same sentence, for has it not been made clear to us all through the works of social scientists and others that Black family life in the United States is the epitome of weakness and decay? This idea then, that there is represented within Black families a residue of strength, of resilience and adaptability, so well documented in this report, deserves some advance consideration.

One question which arises immediately is why has so much attention been given in the literature and most media to the problems Black families face and so little attention to the heroic nature of their grappling with these problems? We have suggested elsewhere that a major reason for this discrepancy is that Black people and Black scholars have had no major hand in drawing these portraits. In this respect then, Dr. Hill's work and that of a handful of other young Black scholars provides a necessary corrective to American scholarship. If we raise the corollary question why so little attention has been paid to the vast majority of Black families while such heavy concentration has been placed on the minority of so-called "female headed families," we come again to a need to understand the strange preoccupations of white social scientists.

Beneath all these matters, however, are four questions which demand our attention and further enlightenment: (1) What are the historical, contemporary and emerging structures of Black family life in America? (2) What are the patterns of functioning which these families have evolved? (3) What is the relationship between family structure and family functioning? (4) What is the relationship between the operation of the political, economic and social forces of the larger society on the one hand and the structure and functioning of Black families on the other? These questions are at the heart of any effort to understand Black families in America today and it might well be that they are also at the heart of any effort to understand the contemporary functioning of the larger social order.

In addressing these issues, young Black social scientists such as Dr. Hill, have an enormous contribution to make to the development of a new social science for it must be clear to the readers of this report that the old social science has not served us well enough. In its failure to describe accurately the experience of Black people, social science has misled us in its description of the larger society. As Lerone Bennett has observed, it is impossible to accurately describe a whole while ignoring or distorting the existence of its essential parts.

The study of family structure in the Black community has been characterized by a plethora of misconceptions. It is widely believed, for example, in some very enlightened circles, that some children have only one parent while some have two and that the Black community is characterized by a high degree of one-parent families. One sometimes wonders whether the social scientists who generate these conceptions ever lived in families or ever lived in the Black community or whether their academic training has blinded them to the realities of their own existence. This is one respect in which scientific sociology has blinded scholars to the realities they would seek to describe. Ralph Ellison has captured the dimensions of this phenomenon:

> If [the Negro] writer accepts the cliches to the effect that the Negro family is usually a broken family, that it is matriarchal in form and that the mother dominates and castrates the males, if he believes that Negro males are having all of these alleged troubles with their sexuality, or that Harlem is a "Negro ghetto" . . . —well, he'll never see the people of whom he wishes to write. . . .[1]

Ellison's observations are not confined to fiction discriptions of black family life. He continues:

> I don't deny that these sociological formulas are drawn from life, but I do deny that they define the complexity of Harlem. . . . I simply don't recognize Harlem in them. And I certainly don't recognize the people of Harlem whom I know. Which is by no means to deny the ruggedness of life there, nor the hardship, the poverty, the sordidness, the filth. But there is something else in Harlem, something subjective, willful, and complexly and compellingly human. It is "that something else" that challenges the sociologists who ignore it, and the society which would deny its existence. It is that "something else" which makes for our strength, which makes for our endurance and our promise.[2]

Dr. Hill's book has made giant strides in reflecting on the varieties and the complexities of which Ralph Ellison speaks. He is not alone. There is a growing body of Black scholars turning their attention to this very basic necessity. Joyce Ladner, in her

[1] "A Very Stern Discipline," interview with Ralph Ellison, *Harper's Magazine* (March 1967), p. 76.
[2] *Ibid.* p. 76.

new book, *Tomorrow's Tomorrow: The Black Woman,* has succeeded in bringing the tools of social inquiry to a most sensitive analysis of the problems and the promise of growing into womanhood in the Black community. Robert Staples, in his new book, *The Black Family: Essays and Studies,* has collected a body of essays and research which portray the strengths as well as the problems of Black families, and which provide documented evidence of the gaps in our knowledge about Black families which gives rise to the need for a new sociology. In his new book, *The Family Life of Black Americans,* Charles V. Willie has shown a similar spectrum of writings. The particular contribution of Dr. Hill's work, however, is that he has relied almost exclusively on national data collected by the most standard sources, including the Census Bureau, the Labor Department, the Department of Health, Education and Welfare, and has brought to these data his keen analytic mind and found within them pictures of life which have been overlooked by less sensitive observers and analysts. It should be clear to all who read this work that the variety of family structures in the Black community cannot be captured by rigid questionnaires based on preconceptions of the investigators which grow out of the white middle-class perspective. Nor can the picture of family structure be determined by who answers the doorbell when the college student comes to call, or by whose name appears on the birth certificate, or by who picks up the welfare check, or by which street corner man boasts the loudest about his progeny. Unfortunately, however, most of our current knowledge about structures of family life have been generated from these mythologies.

It is in the area of family functioning where the creative work of social science is yet to be done. How can we explain, for example, how children are taught to be loving human beings and to have faith in the future by families whom the larger society has almost deserted? Much of social science analysis of Black people is comparative in nature. It compares the intimate details of situations among Black people with those of the white community. The conceptual fallacy of this technique of analysis has seldom been analyzed. Such comparative analysis presupposes that at some point or time in history Black people and white people lived on a basis of equality and were subjected to equal supports and resources from their society. Consequently, any divergence in behavior, attitudes or conditions from this basis of equality and similarity must be explained. Yet we know by the reality of our own lives that no such basis of equality ever existed in this country, but we have developed no tools of analysis that starts with the basis of inequality which has always existed. If we can find our way to do so, this will tell us much more about the kind of society in which we live than the comparative analysis now so common in social science. Then we will find it necessary to explain why so many Black children learn to read rather than why so few do, and how so many Black youth stay out of jail, and how so many Black families manage to be self-supporting, and perhaps how others can be enabled to do likewise. Moreover, this kind of analysis may enable us to translate the strengths of Black families into social science laws for the benefit of the larger society and most importantly of all, this kind of social science analysis based on the realities of our existence rather than a fictional reading of it, may provide a sounder base for the reordering of our society and reordering of our institutions.

A few years ago, Talcott Parson became the high priest of social science by his development of the equilibrium model of social analysis. Parsons is still perhaps the most respected American social scientist, in large part because most other social scientists share his values and his commitment to the status quo. Social change is only a slogan in social science. Elsewhere we have called for the overthrow of the current ruling elite in social science which is largely comprised of white males over forty. It is heartening to see that a number of fresh perspectives of social science are emerging. Dr. Hill's work is a striking example of this new perspective.

When we think about the relationship between family structure and function in the Black community, the misconception is still widespread that the manner in which families function, that is to say how they manage to meet the needs of their members, is determined by the structure of family life. Thus, it is widely argued that two-parent families are inherently stable and one-parent families are inherently unstable. It is widely argued that children in so-called two-parent families do better in school than children of one-parent families, and it is almost universally argued in social science literature that Black families on welfare are there because of the absence of the malfunctioning of the father. Furthermore, the assumption that Black women are more stable economic providers for their families than men has not yet been penetrated. It is very widely argued that Black women are treated better economically than Black men. All these misconceptions grow directly out of the values and the techniques of the best social scientists in the country. They have almost reached the level of absolute laws. And yet, they're all wrong and all contrary to the realities of the Black experience. It is clearly the task of young Black social scientists, who can combine their own experience with their technical competence, to clarify for us the nature of these realities.

For the structure and the function of Black family life together with the nature of the relationship between the two are frought with misconceptions and ignorance. The manner in which the larger society affects these more intimate aspects of family life is subjected to even more distortion, and here the most fundamental misreading is the extent to which the economic, political and social forces of the larger society determine the conditions, the form and the substance of Black family life. The operation of General Motors, the State Department and the Ford Foundation have more to do with the structure and functioning of Black family life than the attitudes, desires and personal proclivities of all the young men and young women who have been the subject of sociological analyses. Black families are more the creatures of their society than its creators. They are in a true sense colonial-type subjects. They are victimized by a careless and malignant society. The policies which govern their lives are determined by others, and they are determined by those who are largely under the influence of a government which is itself largely under the influence of industry. And for at least the last two generations the public social policies of government and industry have been more connected to the destruction of life than to its enhancement. Social science and social scientists have not been immune to the influences of this military-industrial-academic complex. It is perhaps for this reason that from the disinherited, that is, Black youth who have been left out of the conception and operation of their society, may come the new social science.

Dr. Andrew Billingsley
Vice-President for Academic Affairs
Howard University

ACKNOWLEDGMENTS

I wish to convey my thanks to everyone who helped in any way to make this report possible. In particular, I would like to thank the following persons: Andrew Billingsley, Elizabeth Herzog, Joyce A. Ladner, and Robert K. Merton for reveiwing an earlier draft of this report and Hylan Lewis for making available to me important source material. To all of my colleagues in the National Urban League I am grateful. But especially to: Harold Sims, formerly Deputy Executive Director, for his continuous support of our research activities in general and of this report in particular; Betti S. Whaley, Jeweldean Londa and Charles Sharpe for constructively criticizing an earlier draft; and James Williams and his Communications Department staff for outstanding public relations efforts.

Special thanks must go to all the members of the Research Department who, in one way or another, provided invaluable assistance in the preparation of this report: Norma Chapman, Esther Piovia, Althea Williams, Deborah Allen, George Jordan, Barbara Patterson and Dorothy Stewart. I am also grateful to Nathalie Morton for providing needed library assistance.

My deepest appreciation goes to my mentor, Dorothy K. Newman, formerly Director of Research, for opening new research vistas to me and for guiding me in the preparation of this report to insure that a quality effort was achieved.

Finally, I must thank those persons most responsible for strengthening my life: my wife, Joan, for her constant support and encouragement, my minister, Reverend George Lawrence, the dynamic pastor in Brooklyn's Bedford-Stuyvesant, for his social gospel of active concern and involvement in eradicating society's ills; and my parents, Marie and Curtis, for rearing me in a low-income family that, although eventually apart, was always "together."

INTRODUCTION

Most discussions of black families in the literature tend to focus on indicators of instability, disintegration, weakness or pathology. E. Franklin Frazier's monumental work, *The Negro Family in the United States,* is considered to have established this "pejorative tradition" in the study of black families in general and low-income black families in particular.[1] Despite the absence of data in Frazier's works indicating that "disorganized" patterns are characteristic of the majority of low-income blacks, social scientists, such as Glazer and Moynihan, continue to portray low-income black family life as "typically" disorganized, pathological and disintegrating. Others assert that a self-perpetuating "culture of poverty" exists among blacks.[2] But the pejorative perspective of black life patterns is so pervasive that it can be found in the works of some contemporary black scholars as well.[3]

Unfortunately, this traditional focus has created the false impression that instability and pathology are characteristic of *most* black families. There is a tendency to forget that deviance, by definition, refers to departures from the *norm.* Thus, in general, deviance among blacks is as "abnormal" as it is among whites. The great majority of black families, for example, are not characterized by criminality, delinquency, drug addiction or desertion.

This preoccupation with pathology in most research on

1

black families has obscured some fruitful avenues of investigation. Many scholars in this field have failed to realize that a determination of "why most people conform" can help in understanding "why the few deviate." It is our contention that examining the strengths of black families can contribute as much toward understanding and ameliorating some social problems as examining their weaknesses.

Our departure from the "pathological" approach to black family life is an attempt to adopt an earlier perspective evident in the works of Du Bois, Johnson and Drake and Gayton, which has been reasserted by such contemporary scholars as Billingsley, Herzog, Lewis and Valentine:[4]

> . . . we do not view the Negro family as a causal nexus in a tangle of pathology which feeds on itself. Rather, we view the Negro family in theoretical perspective as a subsystem of the larger society. It is, in our view, an absorbing, adaptive, and amazingly resilient mechanism for the socialization of its children and the civilization of its society. (*Billingsley 1968*)

Ladner's (1971) well-documented work, *Tomorrow's Tomorrow*, clearly incorporates Billingsley's perspective. For, while it effectively punctures such cherished notions as the black matriarchy, the emasculation of the black male and the pathological ghetto family, its primary focus is on the strengths and resources of young black women growing up in urban ghettos.

But with few exceptions, most references to the strengths of black families have been oblique. Moreover, black family strengths have not yet been operationally defined and systematically subjected to empirical verification.[5]

If, as most scholars agree, there is a need to strengthen black families, then a first-order priority should be the identification of presently-existing strengths, resources and potentials. Systematic examination of the strengths of black families should facilitate the development of national policies and programs which enhance and use these assets to their fullest potential. It is with these concerns in mind that this report will describe the strengths and resources of black families and demonstrate that strength and stability, not weakness and instability, are the *modal* patterns for both low-income and middle-income black families.

What Are Family Strengths?

Because of the subjectivity of the term, it is not easy to specify what is meant by a "family strength." A strength, according to one set of criteria, could easily be interpreted as a weakness, according to another set of criteria—and vice-versa. For example, most observers would probably agree that a strong bond of affection between members of a family is usually an asset. But if this affection is manifested in homosexual and incestuous relationships among family members, such a bond would generally be characterized as a "pathological" liability.

The classic analysis of the family as a social system by Parsons yield several helpful dimensions of family strengths.[6] One of these dimensions, the ability to provide the necessary functions (both expressive and instrumental) to members and non-members, is basic to a viable family unit. We, therefore, operationally define as family strengths those traits which facilitate the ability of the family to meet the needs of its members and the demands made upon it by systems outside the family unit. They are necessary for the survival and maintenance of effective family networks.

Based upon a survey of what families perceived to be their strengths, Otto (1962) identified several family strengths in his instructive essay, "What Is a Strong Family?" Those traits listed by Otto that are most relevant to our discussion are as follows:

1. A concern for family unity, loyalty and inter-family cooperation.
2. An ability for self-help and the ability to accept help when appropriate.
3. An ability to perform family roles flexibly.
4. An ability to establish and maintain growth-producing relationships within and without the family.

5. The ability to provide for the physical, emotional and spiritual needs of a family.

Examination of the literature on black families reveals that the following characteristics have been functional for their survival, development and stability:

1. Strong kinship bonds
2. Strong work orientation
3. Adaptability of family roles
4. Strong achievement orientation
5. Strong religious orientation

Although these traits can be found among white families, they are manifested quite differently in the lives of black families because of the unique history of racial oppression experienced by blacks in America. In fact, the particular forms that these characteristics take among black families should be viewed as adaptations necessary for survival and advancement in a hostile environment. We shall, therefore, identify these traits as black family strengths. Although many other strengths of black families can and should be identified, we shall restrict our analysis to the five cited above.

Part I

STRONG
KINSHIP
BONDS

According to the literature, low-income families usually have stronger kinship ties than middle-income families. Thus, kinship relations tend to be stronger among black than white families.[7] This can be sharply seen in the higher frequency to which black families take relatives into their households. In most cases, these additional relatives are likely to be children rather than adults.

Absorption of Individuals:
Minors and the Elderly

When we examine census data for families with no children of their own under 18 at home, we find that black families are much more likely than white families to take in other young related members.[8] In husband-wife families, only three percent of white families compared to 13 percent of black families took in relatives under 18. In families headed by a woman, the black families demonstrate an even greater tendency to absorb other related children. Forty-one percent of them, compared to only seven percent of similarly-situated white women, had relatives under eighteen living with them. But the families headed by elderly women take in the highest proportion (48 percent) of children. (*See Table 1*)

About the same proportion of black and white families have

elderly persons living with them, except in families headed by a woman where a higher proportion of white (10 percent) than black (4 percent) families had elderly members. These elderly persons play important roles in many of these families, such as baby-sitting with grandchildren. These services often provide additional income to elderly persons. (*See Table 2*)

We have seen that black families are more likely than white families to take in additional children, while white families are just as likely as black families to have elderly members in their households. And elderly black women are more likely to take children into their own households than be taken into the household of younger kin. But what about the absorption of additional families rather than individuals?

Absorption of Families

According to discussions in the literature, extended family relationships have historically been greater among blacks than whites. At the turn of the century, "doubling-up" was a common occurrence in many black families, particularly among new arrivals to urban areas.[9] Recent Census data relating to subfamilies suggest that a differential between blacks and whites still exists. But these data also indicate that subfamilies are present in a much smaller proportion (6 percent) of black families than is commonly believed. Moreover, the extended family pattern appears to be steadily declining among both black and white families. (*See Table 3*)

Informal Adoption

Since formal adoption agencies have historically not catered to non-whites, blacks have had to develop their own network for the informal adoption of children. This informal adoption network among black families has functioned to tighten kinship bonds, since many black women are reluctant to put their children up for adoption. When they are formally placed, black children are more likely than white children to be adopted by relatives.

While two-thirds of the white babies born out-of-wedlock in 1968 were adopted or placed in foster homes or institutions a year later, only seven percent of the black babies born out-of-wedlock were formally adopted or placed. If we equate the increase in new families headed by a single female between 1968–1969 with the birth of these out-of-wedlock children, we can account for another one-fourth of the white babies, but only three percent of the black babies. This leaves 90 percent of the black babies and only seven percent of the white babies to be informally adopted or retained by already existing families. (*See Table 4*)

The fact that the proportion of new families headed by single women is so much higher for whites than for blacks suggests constraints on white women with out-of-wedlock children to form their own households if they wish to retain their children. One wonders how much increase in families headed by single white women would occur if only 7 percent of their out-of-wedlock children were adopted, as it is for blacks? (Similarly, one wonders how much decrease in informal adoption would occur among blacks if two-thirds of their out-of-wedlock babies were formally adopted, as it is for whites?)

We estimate that more than 160,000 out-of-wedlock black babies were absorbed in 1969 by already existing black families. This absorption helps to minimize the number of new black families headed by single women. This feat of self-help among black families is remarkable when one realizes their precarious economic position. In most cases, it is difficult enough for them to provide adequately for their own children without taking in additional ones. The bonds between relatives in black families must indeed be tight and the value placed upon children very high for such a rate of absorption of additional children to occur so regularly among these families.

These findings also strongly suggest that present placement policies and assumptions of most adoption agencies need to be radically overhauled. The disproportionate number of black children awaiting placement in these agencies is often attributed to the reluctance or "apathy" of blacks to adopt children, but this is not the case. Black families are already adopting children to a very large degree.

In fact, each year black families demonstrate their ability to "adopt" children with a placement rate more than ten times that of formal adoption agencies. (*See Table 5*) Moreover, data from recent studies suggest that black families are even formally adopting children at a greater rate than white families of comparable means.[10] Although we have focused on adoption of out-of-wedlock children, it should be noted that about two-fifths of all black children formally adopted are born "in-wedlock."

Placement regulations of formal adoption agencies would ordinarily prevent most of these families from formally adopting these children. They do not possess the "right" credentials—they are most often "fatherless," or "too poor" or "too disorganized." Since these families demonstrate a capacity to absorb these children each year, innovative placement procedures, such as income subsidies to poor families and placement in families headed by women, should be widely expanded.

It is important to note, however, that illegitimacy is no longer a "growing" problem among blacks. For the illegitimacy rates among blacks have been steadily declining, while the rates among whites have been steadily rising in recent years.[11]

The tight kinship network within black families has proven itself to be an effective mechanism for providing extra emotional and economic support in the lives of thousands of children. These are black family strengths that are clearly in need of support through imaginative adoption policies.

Part II

STRONG
WORK
ORIENTATION

At the beginning of this report, one of the family strengths listed by Otto was "the ability for self-help and the ability to accept help when appropriate." This strength is characteristic of most black families, for contrary to popular conception, black families place a strong emphasis on work and ambition. For example, the black poor still are more likely to work than the white poor: three-fifths of the black poor work, compared to about half of the white poor. (*See Table 6*)

Despite this perseverance, the economic situation of blacks is still a national tragedy: the median family income of blacks is less than two-thirds that of whites; blacks are three times as likely as white to be poor, and black employment rates remain at recession levels, even during periods of "prosperity."[12]

Because families headed by women comprise the majority of families receiving public assistance, it is commonly believed that dependency is characteristic of most of these families. But this is not the case. Recent census data indicate that three-fifths of the women heading black families *work* (most of them full time), although over 60 percent of them are poor. (*See Table 7*) About half of these families receive welfare assistance, thus the majority of them are not completely dependent on welfare. (*See Table 8*)

9

Attitudes Toward Work

Some observers, like Dizard, suggest that blacks are not positively oriented towards work, but are alienated from it. But a number of research findings contradict this notion. In their study of the meanings of work among black and white males, Tausky and Wilson asserted:

> The data reported in this study clearly do not support the alienated type that Dizard has outlined. In fact, only a very small minority of black workers have renounced the widely accepted values of work held in this society. Work estrangement among all status levels is rare indeed and little or no difference exists between the samples of white and black workers. The similarities of work norms between the two groups are exemplified by the fact that 90 percent of the black workers and 91 percent of the white workers indicated that, if out of work, they would rather take a job as a car washer than go on welfare even if the pay for the two sources of income were the same.[13]

The authors also reported that white and black workers were strikingly similar in their desire for work that carries social prestige. An overwhelming majority of both groups want work that is at least respected by the people they know. These results were reinforced by findings from a study of stable working class and middle-class black and white men by Kahl and Goering. That study found a high degree of similarity between blacks and whites on job aspirations and satisfactions, feelings of personal security in employment, as well as certain other work-related attitudes.

Much of the controversy over income assistance plans has resulted from the belief of many national policy-makers that the poor and near-poor do not want to work and, therefore, must be coerced. That is why proposals about work incentive and mandatory work requirements have been included in most family assistance plans. Yet, almost every systematic investigation of work attitudes of low-income persons indicates that mandatory work regulations are not needed to motivate lower status persons to work) Data from current OEO income maintenance experiments confirm (the existence of a strong work orientation among low-income families.[14]

The OEO experiments are being conducted in several cities in New Jersey and one in Pennsylvania to determine the extent to which work disincentives are precipitated by income assistance programs. Many opponents of these programs argued that a significant decline in work activity would occur once these families began receiving supplemental income.

But preliminary findings based on the first eighteen months experience in three cities (Trenton, Paterson and Passaic) and the first twelve months experience in two cities (Jersey City and Scranton) failed to show a significant decline in weekly family earnings as a result of the income assistance program.

About 31 percent of the experimental families and 33 percent of the control families (those of the same kind not getting assistance) showed earnings increases of more than $25 a week during the first year. Also, about 25 percent of income recipients showed declines of more than $25 compared to 23 percent of those families not receiving assistance.

Double Earners

The husband-wife families have been consistently described as the most stable and prosperous of black families. A major source of this strength and "prosperity" is the presence of a working wife in the majority of these families. About two-thirds of the wives in black families work, compared to only half of the wives in white families. (See Table 9)

Since black families have a disproportionate number of working wives, it is misleading to compare—as the Census Bureau recently did—the median incomes of husband-wife families of blacks and whites without taking into account the presence of multiple earners. Such comparisons may, in fact, create an illusion of black families closing income gaps that still remain.[15]

This concern is reinforced by recent census data which indicate that two-earner black families, on the average, still have lower incomes than one earner white families. The median income of black families with two earners in 1969 was $7,782, compared to a median income of $8,450 for white families with only one earner. This is not to say that black two-parent families have not made some gains. But an assessment of the impact of multiple earners is essential for distinguishing apparent gains from substantive ones.

Because the wife is likely to be working in most black families, the fiction that her earnings are often greater than those of her husband has somehow gained widespread currency. This view, which is one of the pillars in the equally widespread belief about "female-dominance" in black families, is even expounded by some of the more perceptive observers such as Ulf Hannerz:

> According to the mainstream model the wife tends to depend on her husband as a provider and he is the family's anchor in the wider society. However, as we noted . . . a rather large number of women in the ghetto are employed, while many of the men are not. This does not mean that more women than men have employment, but in comparison with the wider American society, the job distribution of the ghetto involves relatively more women and fewer men. Thus the contribution to the family of the husband and father as a breadwinner is not only absolutely smaller than it ought to be according to the mainstream model. It is also relatively smaller compared to the contribution of the wife and mother.[16]

Aldous' statements on this matter, however, are more explicit:

> Both camps are in agreement, however, that the abdication of the Negro male from family responsibilities slows progress toward integration . . .

> Given the strong matriarchal tradition within the Negro family and the fact that women can earn much the same amount as lower class husbands, the latter have difficulty solidifying their family position with its attendant rights and responsibilities. The wife's working outside the home

may result in the male's occupying a peripheral family position and abdicating his responsibilities.[17]

The fact is that wives in poor black families contribute less to the total family income than do wives in non-poor black families because they are much less likely to be employed. While ninety percent of the husbands in all black families work, two-thirds of the wives also work. But although 70 percent of the husbands in poor black families work, only 44 percent of the wives work. Thus it is apparent that a working wife is a primary factor in keeping many black families out of poverty. *(See Table 9)*

Despite the frequent assertions about their greater job stability, black women are more likely than black men to be unemployed.[18] Earnings data tell a similar story: just as the earnings of white women are significantly lower than the earnings of white men (even within similar occupational groupings), the earnings of black women are significantly *lower* than the earnings of black men.[19]

Recent data from the Bureau of Labor Statistics also reveal that in over half of the black families in which wives work, they contributed less than *one-third* of family income. And in only 13 percent of these families was the earnings of the wives equal to or greater than their husband's. Therefore, in about 90 percent of the black families with working wives, the earnings of the husband exceeded that of the wife. *(See Table 10)*

Contrary to popular belief, the earnings of wives in low-income black families similarly constitute a small proportion of the total family income. In only fifteen percent of the black families with incomes under $3,000 did the wife's earnings equal or exceed the husband's In fact, in almost half of these families the wife's earnings comprised less than *one-fifth* of the total family income. Thus, in 85 percent of these low-income families, the husband's earnings surpassed the wife's.

Interestingly, however, the data in Table 10 also reveal that wives' earnings are more likely to equal husbands' earnings in low-income white families than in low-income black families. Although the wife's earnings in only fifteen percent of the low-income black families equalled or exceeded the husband's the wife's earnings equalled or exceeded the husband's earnings in one-fourth of the low-income white families! If this can be used as an indicator of "female dominance," then low-income white families can be said to be more "matriarchal" than low-income black families. But our main findings are that the husbands' earnings greatly exceed the wives' in most black and white families.

Although blacks are twice as likely as whites to be unemployed, studies of employment histories in black communities reveal a high degree of job stability among the majority of black men. In a recent study of black and white male workers, for example, Kahl and Goering found that almost 80 percent of the blacks compared to 60 percent of the whites had held their current jobs for at least three years. And almost one-half of the blacks but only a third of the whites had held their jobs for ten years or more![20]

Contrary to the stereotypes of "irresponsible," "peripheral" and "chronically unemployed" that abound in the literature, the husband is the main provider in the overwhelming majority of black families, both poor and non-poor.[21]

It is sometimes asserted that the "greater" earnings ability of the black woman over the black man is due to her higher level of education. Although the median years of schooling for black women (10.4) is still somewhat higher than it is for black men (10.0), their educational levels have been sharply converging in recent years. More importantly, however, the historically lower occupations held by black women due to sex discrimination, alone, more than undermined any "superiority" in the earnings sphere they might have held over black men because of a slightly higher educational level.[22]

In sum, the data presented above indicate that a strong work orientation exists among blacks, as it does among most Americans. And, self-help is the characteristic pattern of most black families. They do not have to be coerced to work; the only work incentive needed is a decent job at decent wages. In the majority of black families, wives provide needed additional economic, as well as emotional, support. Although their earnings fall far below their husbands' the additional income contributed by the wives is essential for the survival and stability of many of these families. And, in the overwhelming majority of black families, whether poor or not, the husband assumes the primary responsibility of breadwinner.

Part III

ADAPTABILITY
OF FAMILY
ROLES

In discussing another family strength, the ability to perform family roles flexibly, Otto observed:

> It is a strength when family members can "fill in" and assume each other's roles as needed. For example, a father can function as a "mother" and children can temporarily be "parents" to their father and mother.[23]

Such flexibility of family roles exists in many black families and is a source of strength and stability. Much of this role flexibility probably developed in response to economic necessities. Because of the high proportion of working wives in black families, it is common for older siblings to act as "parents" of younger siblings. Moreover, many black youngsters have to enter the labor market early to supplement the family income. In many two-parent black families, especially those with working wives, occasions often arise that require the wife to act as the "father" or the husband as the "mother." Such role flexibility helps to stabilize the family in the event of an unanticipated separation (because of death, divorce, separation or a sustained illness) of the husband, wife, or other key family members, for example. In most black families, there is much sharing of decisions and tasks.[24]

Equalitarian Family Patterns

Although the literature is replete with references to a "matriarchal tradition" among black families, most empirical data suggest that an "equalitarian" pattern is characteristic of most black families. Interestingly, supporting data for an equalitarian pattern among black families can be found in the one empirical investigation cited by Moynihan to support his thesis of a pervasive black matriarchy.[25]

That study by Blood and Wolfe concluded that "female dominance" was the representative pattern of most two-parent black families. But examination of that work reveals that the data were misinterpreted. This can be seen in the authors' scoring of their "power" scale: scores below 4 indicated "wife dominance," scores from 4 through 6 indicated an "equalitarian" family in which both parents shared power, and scores over 6 indicated "husband dominance." But the average power score for white families was 5.2, while the average power score for black families was 4.4. Consequently, *both* black and white families, on the average, reported equalitarian patterns. Although it is true that the average score for black families was *skewed* toward "wife dominance," the fact remains that the characteristic pattern for the *average* two-parent black family was equalitarian.

Data from a recent analysis by Hyman and Reed also suggest that an equalitarian (rather than a "matriarchal") pattern is the modal pattern for most black two-parent families.[26] In a secondary analysis of national survey data, they found virtually no differences between the responses about family decision-making among blacks and whites. For example, in response to a question about who makes the important family decisions, among blacks, 28 percent said it was the father, compared to only 14 percent who said it was the mother. Similar results were obtained for whites: 23 percent said it was the father, while 13 percent said it was the mother. The fact that a majority of blacks and whites failed to choose either parent suggests that "both" was a more common response; thus an equalitarian family pattern is implied.

Similar findings resulted when a national sample of married Americans were asked who made the important decisions in their families. Among blacks, nine percent said it was the husband, while ten percent said it was the wife. Among whites, six percent said it was the husband and seven percent said it was the wife. Again, an equalitarian pattern is suggested since over 80 percent of both black and white couples did not choose either of the two alternatives.

A study of family decision-making by Middleton and Putney also found the equalitarian pattern to be characteristic among both blacks and whites:

> Thus we find no evidence that whites and Negroes, profes-
> sors and skilled workers, differ as to which spouse dominates
> in the making of daily decisions. Contrary to the literature,
> our data suggest that all these groups are predominantly
> equalitarian.[28]

Further empirical support for an equalitarian pattern among low-income black families in particular comes from another study purporting to support the Moynihan thesis. This study by Joan Aldous, based on a sample of lower-class married black and white men, examined the extent to which these men reported that they and their wives participated in family decision-making and performing household tasks.[29] The investigator was interested in observing the differential participation of men with employed and unemployed wives.

The mean scores for the performance of ten household tasks (as reported by the husbands) are listed in Table 11. These indicate that, in general, there is a great degree of similarity between lower-class white and black husbands in their performance of household tasks. Both groups of men, for example, indicate that they—and not their wives—most often borrow money, take clothes to the laundry and discipline children. Black men tend to take out garbage more often than white men, while white men tend to shop for groceries somewhat more often than black men.

The implications of these findings for family patterns can be more easily interpreted by collapsing the data in the format indicated in Table 12. It becomes immediately evident that in the majority of lover-class black families an equalitarian pattern predominates, whether the wife is working or not. But among lower-class white families, an equalitarian pattern is characteristic of those families with unemployed wives, while a "matriarchal" pattern seems to be most prevalent among those white families with working wives. Thus the employed wives in the white families in this study received the least assistance from their husbands.[30]

In their study of a representative community sample of married black males, Parker and Kleiner were somewhat surprised to find no significant psychological discrepancies between the men's reports about the "ideal" and "actual" decision-making and task performances patterns in their families.[31] Contrary to the authors' expectations, over 80 percent of the men reported that they "almost always" or "usually" (a) make the decisions in money and other important family matters (b) share the responsibility of financially supporting the household with their wives; (c) share the responsibility of training their children; and (d) talk to their wives about things that bother them.

The men's self-reports certainly do not fit the literature's stereotypes of "peripheral," "weak" and "hen-pecked" husbands. It is imperative, as Ladner notes, to distinguish between "dominant" and "strong" wives. She asserts that although most black wives are strong, they are not domineering. It is the constant confusion of strength with dominance that helps to perpetuate the matriarch image among black families.

In sum, the available data suggest that the "typical" family pattern among black families is equalitarian and not "matriarchal." Moreover, the husbands in most black families are actively involved in decision-making and the performance of household tasks that are expected of them. And most wives, while strong, are not dominant matriarchs, but share with their husbands the making of family decisions—even in the low-income black families.[32]

One-parent families

The higher proportion of families headed by women among blacks is taken as an indicator of disorganization and instability. But it need not be so. The self-reliance of black women who are the primary breadwinners of their families best exemplifies this adaptability of family roles. The low remarriage rate among these women can partly be explained by the greater self-confidence they have in being able to function as the head of the family. *(See Table 16)* Because of many stabilizing factors in families that are headed by women, there is no need to assume a "pathological" functioning to these families. As Merton observes, many forms of deviation may, in fact, be normal, healthy responses to particular social environments:

> Our primary aim is to discover how some social structures exert a definite pressure upon certain persons in the society to engage in non-conforming rather than conforming conduct. If we can locate groups peculiarly subject to such pressures, we should expect the fairly high rates of deviant behavior in these groups, not because the human beings comprising them are compounded of destructive biological tendencies, but because they are responding normally to the social situation in which they find themselves . . . Should our quest be at all successful, some forms of deviant behavior will be found to be as psychologically normal as conformist behavior, and the equation of deviation and psychological abnormality will be put in question.[33]

Although greater attention is generally given to the "pathology" of families headed by women by scholars, several investigators have obtained results that reveal a wide range of functioning patterns in many of these families. In his study of child-rearing practices among low-income families, Lewis observed:

> The materials and analysis of the Child Rearing Study point to wide variety in the styles of individuals and fam-

ilies. They show that all low-income people are not lower class in orientations to life and in showing the preferences conventionally ascribed to this category . . . Our field experience in Washington suggests that it is highly questionable that all or even a substantial majority of the low-income (lower-class) "female-based" households among Negroes are responsive to and supporters of a destructively organized or integrated way of life.[34]

It should not be inferred from our discussion of the adaptability of one-parent families that this family form is a preferred pattern among blacks or that it has no problems functioning. On the contrary, for this role, as Herzog so aptly describes it, is a very difficult one:

Few would deny that it is a difficult and demanding role. For many, it is a dual role, as homemaker-child-rearer and as breadwinner. By definition, it is a role that must be enacted without the psychological and physical support of a parent partner to help with household responsibilities, family decisions, and all that child rearing involves. For many, it includes reduction in income, social status and social activities, posing a struggle against resentment, isolation and self-doubt.[35]

Our aim is to underscore the importance of systematically assessing the functioning patterns of different kinds of families instead of prejudging their adequacy on the basis of moral judgments. In other words, because two-parent families are preferred in American society over one-parent families is no justification for assuming that all two-parent families function "positively." In fact, investigations have found many one-parent families that function better than many two-parent families.[36]

It is commonly believed that the negative impact of one-parent families, especially on male children, is a demonstrated fact. But, as a careful review of the literature on boys in fatherless families by Herzog and Sudia reveals, the data supporting this belief are far from conclusive.[37] Because of sharp differences and deficiencies in the research design of many of these investigations, the conclusions reached are often contradictory, tenuous, and of dubious relevance to black youth in American ghettos.

For example, one of the most frequently cited studies purporting to show the adverse effects of father absence is a study of Norwegian, not American, families. And the fathers in those families studied were sailors whose absences were not permanent, but were temporary and recurrent. (This investigation was carefully replicated in a study of Italian families that emerged with contradictory findings.) Since, as Herzog and Sudia point out, much of the research on boys in fatherless families has involved father absences that are sanctioned or honorable, the effect of father absences which are morally disapproved (such as desertion or divorce) remains to be systematically examined. The methodological weaknesses (and strengths) of most of this literature is discussed in detail by Herzog and Sudia. One weakness, the lack of comparison between the functioning patterns of two-parent and one-parent families, was central to almost all of these investigations.[38]

Aug and Bright tried to overcome this shortcoming in an interesting investigation of illegitimacy.[39] They attempted to test whether one-parent families with out-of-wedlock children were more "pathological" than two-parent families with "in-wedlock" children. Extensive interviews were conducted with groups of young married and unwed mothers, consisting largely of Appalachian whites and blacks from the Bluegrass region of Kentucky.

They found a high degree of normal psychosocial development in those families with out-of-wedlock children that had the support of other family members and relatives. Such families functioned better than many two-parent families with "in-wedlock" children. However, in those "out-of-wedlock families" (especially the white ones) where additional support from family members or relatives was not forthcoming, the functioning was seriously impaired. Thus, Aug and Bright concluded:

> Most works on illegitimacy have ignored legitimate pregnancy in similar groups of people . . . If the unwed mothers

are selected from a population which has a high baseline
of psychopathology, one could easily get a distorted view
of the "problems" of these people . . . A control group,
however, might well show that many of the problems seen
are widely distributed through the subculture, so that they
are coincidental to, rather than directly related to, illegitimacy. In the data which we have presented, it is seen that
the "problem" of disturbed interpersonal relationships is
well-represented in both wed and unwed groups. It therefore seems that it would be wise to take a broad look at the
entire subculture if one is to assess the import of illegitimacy as a "problem" or as a symptom of "problems" for a
particular group.[40]

The results of investigations by Banglow and others also revealed that, out-of-wedlock pregnancy, far from being the beginning of a downhill spiral, may be an important factor leading to
increased depth of understanding between the unwed mother
and her family of origin. The extent of support or rejection by
family members and relatives was a crucial factor in the functioning of these parents. The study by Aug and Bright indicated
that support from the extended family was more likely to be
found among blacks than whites in families with out-of-wedlock
children. These results reinforce our findings on the strong kinship bonds among black families.[41]

Although there is much discussion about the "pathological"
or "disorganized" functioning of families, it is surprising to find
that very little work has been done in operationalizing the concept of "family functioning" to apply to the family as a system.
This is true of two-parent as well as one-parent families. The
typical approach has been, in examining the effects of one-parent
families, to make inferences about negative functioning on the
basis of the extent of deviant attitudes or behavior exhibited by
particular children.

In one of those rare approaches, Geismar and Ayres developed the St. Paul Scale of Family Functioning.[42] This scale
was specifically designed to assess the adequacy of family functioning of low-income families in nine major categories: house-

hold practices, health conditions, economic practices, social activities, community resources, worker relationships, family relationships, individual behavior and child care.

The scale was used on a random sample of black, white and Puerto-Rican families as part of the Rutgers Family Life Improvement Project, a longitudinal study of the social functioning of some 500 urban families.[43] After comparing the functioning levels of the different ethnic groups, holding class constant, Geismar and Gerhart reported no statistically significant differences between the functioning of black and white families.

Desertion

In most discussions of black families headed by women, references to "deserting" husbands are invariably made to partly account for the separation. The view most often expressed is that because black men are unable to adequately provide for their families, they often desert so that the family can qualify for welfare.[44]

It is interesting to note that this desertion thesis is quite popular, despite the almost complete absence of data on desertions to support it. Although some studies have obtained court data which suggest that the probability of desertion is greater among blacks than whites, data on desertion rates are rarely presented to account for the origin of fatherless families.[45] Uninformed inferences about deserting husbands are based primarily on the Census Bureau's marital status category of "separation"—since the Bureau collects no data on desertion rates.

The most readily available nationwide data on desertions are compiled by the National Center for Social Statistics in connection with their national study of AFDC families. As the data in Table 13 reveal, in only one-fifth of the black AFDC families was the status of the father characterized as "deserted."[46]

When the father-present families are excluded, as indicated in Table 14, the total of the proportions of "separated" and "deserted" black AFDC families is 41 percent. Thus, the deserted families account for only one-half of the families that would be classified as "separated" or "other" in Census Bureau marital status categories. Comparisons between the marital statuses of black AFDC and all black families reveal marked differences. They suggest that since the majority of "separated" AFDC families are not classified as "deserted," the majority of separated families headed by women in general should not be similarly classified without empirical verification.

Suicide Rates

In most discussions of the pathology of black families, a significant indicator of alienation, suicide rates, is rarely mentioned. Why is this so? Is it that the rates are in the "wrong" direction? Since suicide rates are much higher among whites than blacks, they fail to fit conveniently the theories of self-hatred and pathology that social scientists have generated about blacks.

It is particularly interesting to note that the suicide rates are lowest among black women, a group that continually experiences adversity. Black women have a suicide rate of 2.4 compared to a suicide rate of 6.3 among white women. And the rate for black males is 7.3, compared to the rate of 16.9 for white males. (See Table 15)

The lower susceptibility to suicide among blacks—a possible indicator of stability—is an intriguing area for further analysis.

In this section, we have discussed various forms of adaptation in two-parent and one-parent black families. We have tried to delineate various sources of stability in both kinds of families. There is a need to systematically examine the relative strengths and weaknesses of black and white families of both types.

Part IV

HIGH ACHIEVEMENT ORIENTATION

One of the unheralded strengths of blacks is the strong achievement orientation of low-income black families. This aspect has been analyzed as mainly leading to frustration or otherwise held as unimportant or overlooked because of methodological biases.

Many of the studies in the literature fail to note the broad range of values and life-styles among persons within similar socio-economic levels and the great similarity of values between persons at different socio-economic levels. This failure is due primarily to methodological biases of many social scientists: (1) the practice of focusing on proportions rather than absolute numbers and (2) focusing on unrepresentative rather than representative proportions. Merton took note of this methodological bias in his critique of Hyman's essay, "The Value Systems of Different Classes":

> ... But what Hyman fails to note, in his otherwise instructive and useful collation of the evidence, is that ... it is *not* the *relative proportions* of the several social classes adopting the cultural goal of success that matter, but their *absolute numbers*. To say that a larger *percentage* of the upper social and economic strata hold fast to the cultural goal of success is not to say that larger numbers of them than of the lower-class people do so. Indeed, since the number of people in the topmost stratum identified in these

studies is substantially smaller than the number in the lowest stratum, it is sometimes the case that more lower-class than upper-class people abide by this goal.[47]

This point was reaffirmed by Merton in another discussion on a related topic:

> It has been repeatedly found that the upper social and educational strata have a relatively higher proportion of "geniuses" or "talents." But since the numbers in these strata are small, the great bulk of geniuses or talents actually come from lower social strata. From the standpoint of the society, of course, it is the absolute numbers and not the proportion coming from any given social stratum which matters.[48]

This oversight applies to many studies that have found the achievement goals and values of the middle-class to be significantly higher than those of the working-class or lower-class.

Although Merton stressed the importance of examining absolute numbers as well as proportions, there is also a need for more social scientists to focus on representative rather than unrepresentative proportions when they generalize about "typical" class or group patterns. Quite often an investigator will focus on the significance of the difference between two unrepresentative proportions and interpret these minority proportions as representing the majority of a group or class stratum. For example, in most discussions about black families, greatest attention is usually given to the significance of the differences between the proportion of female-headed families among whites (9 percent) and the proportion among blacks (28 percent). Most generalizations about the "typical" black family as matriarchal have been based on the differences between these two unrepresentative minority proportions. The fact that husband-wife families represent the overwhelming majority of black families (since it is prevalent in over 70 percent of black families) has usually not deterred many references to a "matriarchy" as being the "typical" pattern of black families.[49]

Johnson and Leslie noted this methodological shortcoming

in a review of the research on class differences in child-rearing practices:

> The understandable tendency of many researchers in this area to stress statistically significant class differences after having generally reported the overall similarities seemingly has aided in the development of what may be unwarranted class images. We contend that this results not only from over-reliance on statistical differences without representative proportions, but from the uncritical use in secondary sources of these more interesting differences to the relative exclusion of overall similarities and the researcher's qualifying statements . . .

> The uncritical acceptance by social scientists of current conceptions of class-linked child-rearing patterns may restrict and render sterile future studies of the variations that should exist in a complex society.[50]

Johnson and Leslie's observations about the tendency of social scientists to create unwarranted class images cannot be overemphasized because of the common practice of equating class correlates, such as income, education, or occupation, with class styles of life or values. This is most likely to occur when an investigator forgets that income is only a *correlate* of class life-styles or values and treats it as if it were synonymous with the concept. He really believes that all "middle-income" persons are "middle-class" and all "low-income" persons are "lower-class," and fails to realize that many low-income persons have "middle-class" values and life-styles, while many middle-income persons have "lower-class" values and life-styles. The belief in the homogeneity of life-styles and values of persons occupying similar socio-economic levels, which is so prevalent in the literature on social class, results partly from this merger of class life styles with their operational indicators.[51]

Our observations apply, of course, to much of the discussion about class differentials in academic orientation. It has been amply documented in the literature that the college aspirations and plans of middle-income students tend to be higher than those of low-income students. It is often forgotten that although a higher *proportion* of middle-income than low-income students have college aspirations, the *majority* of low-income students (and their parents) have college aspirations. Moreover, since blacks from low status families tend to outnumber those in middle status families, the number of black students attending college from low-income families often equals or surpasses the number attending college from middle-income families. For example, an official of Howard University, a black university with an elitist reputation, recently reported that only 19 percent of its students come from homes where at least one parent attended college, more than half come from broken homes, and about 80 percent require some financial support to remain in school.

The remarkable educational advances of large numbers of blacks from deprived backgrounds are also reflected in a recent nationwide survey of college freshmen conducted by the American Council on Education. According to that survey, more than half of the freshmen entering predominantly black institutions come from homes in which the father had not even completed high school, and 80 percent of them come from homes in which the father had not gone to college.[52] Thus, contrary to popular belief, the overwhelming majority of black college students do not come from so-called "middle-class" homes with college-educated parents.

Recent census data on educational attainment provide additional support on the educational achievement of black youth from low status families. According to the October 1970 Current Population Survey, three-fourths of the blacks enrolled in college come from homes in which the family heads had no college education.[53] (*See Table 17*)

In trying to trace the source of the higher educational aspirations among the working-class blacks, Hindelang asked the students to indicate how far they thought their parents wanted them to go to school. While 64 percent of the white students said that their parents wanted them to finish college, a significantly higher proportion (80 percent) of the black students said that their parents wanted them to finish college.[54]

The strong achievement pressures from parents in lower status black families were revealed in several other studies as well. In an investigation of the influences on college attendance, Harris found that among higher status students, a higher percentage of white than black students reported being influenced by their parents.[55] But among lower status students, the proportion reporting that their parents influenced their college attendance was higher among blacks than whites. Moreover, although parental influence increased with status among whites, there was almost no difference in the extent of parental influence reported between higher status and lower status blacks of the same sex. About 75 percent of the black males and about 90 percent of the black women—regardless of status—indicated that their college attendance was influenced by their parents. (*See Table 18*)

In a large-scale study of about 6,000 students attending high schools in the Deep South, Cosby found that lower status blacks had higher occupational aspirations than lower status whites, while higher status whites had higher aspirations than higher status blacks.[56] Findings from this study also suggest the presence of strong achievement pressures on black students in broken families. For the occupational aspirations of black students from lower status broken homes were as high, if not somewhat higher, than the occupational aspirations of black students coming from lower status intact homes. More importantly, the occupational aspirations of blacks from lower status *broken* families were significantly higher than the aspirations of whites from lower status *intact* families. (*See Table 19*)

According to data on college students compiled by the American Council on Education, black students had lower dropout rates, in general, than had been estimated.[57] And, the dropout rates of white males in white colleges were higher than the dropout rates for black males in white colleges, but equalled the dropout rates for black males in black colleges. Among women students, however, although the dropout rates for white

women in white colleges equalled the rates for black women
in black colleges, the dropout rates of black women at white
colleges were significantly higher than the rates for the other
group. (*See Table 20*)

Our findings indicate that an achievement orientation already exists in many low-income black families. These strengths
need to be built upon by truly making education the avenue for
success which the "American Dream" says it ought to be.[58]

Part V

RELIGIOUS ORIENTATION

A strength of black families that has been widely discussed, but less frequently empirically documented, is their strong religious orientation.[59]

Blacks have been adept at using religion as a mechanism for survival and advancement throughout their history in America. During slavery, religion served as a stimulant for hundreds of rebellions that took place. It was also a major source of strength during the civil rights movement of the '50's and the '60's.[60]

But it was through the Negro church, one of the most independent institutions in the black community, that blacks learned to use religion as a survival mechanism. Black ministers frequently used their sermons to transmit coded messages to the congregation. Negro spirituals were often used for similar purposes, particularly in assisting runaway slaves.[61]

One advocate of the black church expressed its historic role as follows:

> In both the Negro and white community, the Negro church has often been made a joke, but the fact is that it's the most organized thing in the Negro's life. Whatever you want to do in the Negro community, whether it's selling Easter Seals or organizing a nonviolent campaign, you've got to do it through the Negro church, or it doesn't get done.

There's no way to tell what would have happened to the Negro if he had not had the church. I'll say flatly that if there had been no Negro church, there would have been no civil rights movement today.[62]

According to a national survey conducted by Louis Harris, over 60 percent of the blacks felt that the black church and minister were helping the cause of blacks somewhat or a lot. Seventeen percent felt, however, that the black church was only helping a little or not at all, while the remaining one-fifth was uncertain.[63]

Although these findings indicate that a majority of blacks hold positive views about the black church, they also suggest much ambivalence or outright hostility on the part of a sizable minority. This rejection of the black church is most evident among black youth today. They are disillusioned by the fact that the overwhelming majority of black churches have only a peripheral involvement in the secular and economic needs of the black community.[64]

Consequently, many grassroot organizations are assuming functions formerly performed by the black church. At the same time, churches with activist ministers are increasingly taking on secular activities, and collaborating with local community action organizations of varying ideologies.

The achievements of the Reverend Leon Sullivan, who was recently elected to General Motors' Board of Directors, may be a harbinger of the kind of adaptations that the contemporary black church must make if it is to remain in the vanguard of the black struggle.[65]

It was on the basis of the effective three-year boycott (1959–62) against Philadelphia merchants by Reverend Sullivan, with the assistance of 400 ministers, that Dr. Martin Luther King, Jr. decided to form Operation Breadbasket as the economic arm of the Southern Christian Leadership Conference.

Moreover, the Opportunities Industrialization Center (OIC), one of the first community-sponsored job training programs, grew out of the small contributions of Sullivan's parishioners. Today O.I.C. Centers have spread out to a hundred cities throughout the nation as well as to the Dominican Republic and Nigeria. During the seven years of its existence, about 65,000 minority persons are said to have been trained for jobs of varying degrees of sophistication.

Fortunately, increasing numbers of young ministers, like the Reverend Jesse Jackson, are also expounding the social gospel of Dr. King and Reverend Sullivan and influencing the lives of thousands of blacks.[66]

Part VI
SUMMARY

Most discussions of black families tend to focus on indicators of instability and weakness. With few exceptions, most social scientists continue to portray black families as disorganized, pathological and disintegrating.

This preoccupation with pathology in most research on black families has obscured some fruitful avenues of investigation. We contend that examining the strengths of black families can contribute as much towards understanding and ameliorating social problems as examining their weaknesses.

If, as most scholars agree, there is a need to strengthen black families, then a first-order priority should be the identification of presently-existing strengths and resources. The National Urban League recognized this need three years ago when it issued a position statement on black families based on the work of Dr. Andrew Billingsley.

This report identifies and analyzes five strengths of black families: adaptability of family roles, strong kinship bonds, strong work orientation, strong religious orientation and strong achievement orientation. These five characteristics have been functional for the survival, advancement and stability of black families. Some of the major findings from this report are as follows:

1. Contrary to the widespread belief in a "matriarchy" among blacks, our findings reveal that most black families, whether low-income or not, are characterized by an equalitarian pattern in which neither spouse dominates, but shares decision-making and the performance of expected tasks.

2. National earnings data do not support the popular conception that wives' earnings in most low-income black families are often greater than the husbands'. Recent Bureau of Labor Statistics data indicate that in 85 percent of the black families with incomes under $3,000, the husband's earnings surpassed the wife's. Thus, contrary to the stereotypes of black men as "weak," "irresponsible," and "peripheral," the husband is the main provider in the overwhelming majority of black families, whether low-income or not.

3. Most black babies born out-of-wedlock are kept by parent and relatives, while most white babies born out-of-wedlock are given away. In 1969, about 90 percent of the black babies born out-of-wedlock, compared to only 7 percent of the white babies born out-of-wedlock, were kept by the parent and kin in existing families. On the other hand, 67 percent of the out-of-wedlock white babies, but only 7 percent of the out-of-wedlock black babies were formally adopted or placed.

4. Contrary to the belief that dependency is characteristic of most families headed by women, recent Census Bureau data indicate that three-fifths of the women heading black families work—most of them full-time.

5. Our study found that most assertions about widespread desertion in black families are not based on actual desertion rates. In fact, recent HEW data reveal that not even the majority of AFDC families can be characterized as "deserted": only one-fifth of the black families receiving AFDC in 1969 were so described.

6. The high achievement orientation of low-income black families is reflected in the large numbers of college students from these families that attend college. For example, three-fourths of the blacks enrolled in college in 1970 came from

homes in which the family heads had no college education. Thus the overwhelming majority of black college students do not come from so-called "middle-class" homes with college-educated parents.

TABLES

Table 1

*Percent of Related Members Under 18 in Families
with No Children of Own Under 18
by Race, Age of Head and Type of Family, March 1970*

Type of Family and Age of Head	Percent with Members under 18 Black	White
Husband-wife families		
All families	13	3
Head under 35	2	3
Head 35–44	7	2
Head 45–64	16	3
Head 65 and over	14	3
Families with female heads		
All families	41	7
Head under 35	24*	17*
Head 35–44	42*	10
Head 45–64	40	13
Head 65 and over	48	10

* Base under 75,000

SOURCE: Prepared by National Urban League Research Department from data in U.S. Department of Commerce, Bureau of the Census, Current Population Reports, Population Characteristics, *Household and Family Characteristics, March 1970,* Series P-20, No. 218, March 23, 1971, Tables 3 and 4.

Table 2

Number and Percent of Relatives over 64 in Families
with Heads under 65, 1970

Type of Family and Age of Head	Black Number (000's)	Percent	White Number (000's)	Percent
Husband-wife families				
Heads under 65	2,923	100	35,530	100
Members over 64	117	4	1,233	3
Heads 45–64	1,194	100	15,286	100
Members over 64	91	8	951	6
Families with female head				
Heads under 65	1,194	100	3,234	100
Members over 64	48	4	328	10
Heads 45–64	401	100	1,614	100
Members over 64	42	10	266	16

SOURCE: Prepared by National Urban League Research Department from data in U.S. Bureau of the Census, *Current Population Reports, Population Characteristics,* "Household and Family Characteristics: March 1970," Series P-20, Number 218, March 23, 1971, Tables 3 and 4.

Table 3

Subfamilies as Percent of All Families
by Race, 1960–1970
(Numbers in thousands)

Race of Head	1960	1970
Black families*	4,262	4,774
Subfamilies	317	268
Percent of total	7	6
White families	40,887	46,022
Subfamilies	1,111	866
Percent of total	3	2

* 1960 figures for blacks include other nonwhite

SOURCE: Prepared by National Urban League Research Department from data in U.S. Bureau of the Census: *U.S. Census of Population: 1960,* "Families," PC(2)-4A, Tables 19 and 22; and *Current Population Reports, Population Characteristics,* "Household and Family Characteristics: March 1970," March 23, 1971, Tables 11 and 12.

Table 4

Imputed Effect of Out-of-Wedlock Births on Family Formation
by Color, 1968–1969

(Numbers in thousands)

Disposition of Children	Black[1]		White	
	Number	*Percent*	*Number*	*Percent*
Out-of-wedlock births (1968)	184	100	155	100
Formally adopted (1969)	12	7	97	62
Foster care or institutionalized[2]	1	3	7	5
Retained in new family[4]	5	3	40	26
Informally adopted or retained in existing families[5]	165	90	11	7

1 The racial statistics on illegitimate births, adoption and foster care apply to nonwhites and not only to blacks.

2 These numbers were obtained by multiplying the increase (8,000) in the number of children in foster care or institutions between 1968 and 1969 by the proportion (12 percent) of nonwhite children estimated by the Children's Bureau to be in homes for dependent or neglected children.

3 Less than 0.5 percent.

4 These numbers represent the increase in families with a single woman as the head between 1968 and 1969. For the purposes of this presentation, it is assumed that each of these new families resulted from the birth of an out-of-wedlock child in 1968.

5 By "informal adoption," we include both (1) the retention of out-of-wedlock children by mothers in already-existing families and (2) the absorption of out-of-wedlock children by such relatives as grandmothers and aunts or by non-relatives.

SOURCE: Prepared by the National Urban League Research Department from data in U.S. National Center for Social Statistics, *Adoptions in 1969: Supplement to Child Welfare Statistics—1969;* U.S. National Center for Health Statistics, *Vital Statistics of the U.S.: 1968, Volume I—Natality;* U.S. Children's Bureau, *America's Children and Youth in Institutions, 1950–1960–1964;* U.S. Census Bureau, *Current Population Reports, Population Characteristics,* "Selected Characteristics of Persons and Families: March 1970," Series P-20, No. 204, July 13, 1970.

Table 5

Proportion of Out-of-Wedlock Children Adopted
Within One Year After Birth
by Race and Year of Birth, 1963–1969
(Numbers in thousands)

Year of Birth of Out-of-Wedlock Children	Black*			White		
	Number out-of-wedlock births	*Number adopted within one year*	*Percent adopted*	*Number out-of-wedlock births*	*Number adopted within one year*	*Percent adopted*
1962	150.4	7.5	5	94.7	62.6	66
1963	150.7	8.0	5	102.2	74.4	73
1964	161.3	9.0	6	114.3	79.0	69
1965	167.5	9.8	6	123.7	86.0	70
1966	169.5	10.0	6	132.9	89.5	67
1967	175.8	10.5	6	142.2	94.0	66
1968	183.9	12.5	7	155.2	96.9	62

* Includes other nonwhites

SOURCE: Prepared by Research Department of the National Urban League from data in U.S. National Center for Social Statistics, *adoptions: Supplements to Child Welfare Statistics*, 1963–1969; and U.S. National Center for Health Statistics, *Vital Statistics of the U.S.: 1968, Volume I—Natality.*

Table 6

Work Status of Heads of Families Below Poverty Level
by Race, 1969

	Black		White	
	Number (000's)	*Percent*	*Number (000's)*	*Percent*
Total poor family heads	1,326	100	3,553	100
Heads who worked	785	59	1,883	53
Heads who did not work	541	41	1,670	47

SOURCE: Prepared by National Urban League Research Department from data in U.S. Department of Commerce, Bureau of the Census, Special Tabulations for OEO from March 1970 Current Population Survey based on 1969 work status and income.

Table 7

Work Experience of Women* Heading Families by Race and Poverty Status, 1969

	Black		White	
	Total families	*Total poor families*	*Total families*	*Total poor families*
Total number (ooo's)	1,349	718	4,185	1,063
Total percent	100	100	100	100
Year round, full time	27	12	32	5
Part year, full time	17	18	15	19
Worked part time	17	19	11	15
Did not work at all	39	50	41	61

* 14 years and over

SOURCE: Prepared by Research Department of the National Urban League from tabulations prepared for U.S. Office of Economic Opportunity from March 1970 Current Population Survey, Tables 3a and 3b.

Table 8

Proportion of Families Headed by Women Receiving AFDC by Race, 1969

(Numbers in thousands)

	Black	White
Total families headed by women	1,327	4,053
AFDC families headed by women	657	584
Percent	50	14

SOURCE: Prepared by Research Department of the National Urban League from data in U.S. Bureau of the Census, "Selected Characteristics of Persons and Families: March 1970," *Current Population Reports: Population Characteristics*, Series P-20, No. 204; and unpublished data from U.S. National Center for Social Statistics based on its 1969 AFDC national study.

Table 9

*Work Experience of Male Heads and Spouses in Black Families
by Poverty Status, 1969*

(Numbers in thousands)

	Total Black Families		Poor Black Families	
	Male heads	*Female spouses*	*Male heads*	*Female spouses*
Total number of families	3,425	3,217	609	563
Total percent	100	100	100	100
In armed forces	2	—	*	—
Year round, full time	64	26	32	6
Part year, full time	17	22	22	17
Part time	6	17	17	21
No work at all	10	35	29	56

* Less than 0.5 percent

SOURCE: Prepared by Research Department of the National Urban League from data in tabulations prepared for U.S. Office of Economic Opportunity from March 1970 Current Population Survey.

Table 10

*Percent of Total Family Income Contributed by Working Wife
in Nonfarm Husband-Wife Families, 1969*

(Families in which wife had paid work experience
during the year. Annual averages.)

Percent of Family Income from Wife's Earnings	All Family Income Groups		Family Income Groups under $3,000	
	*Black**	*White*	*Black**	*White*
Total family income	100	100	100	100
Less than 20 percent	33	38	47	46
20–29 percent	20	19	19	13
30–39 percent	18	19	8	13
40–49 percent	16	12	11	4
50 percent and over	13	11	15	25

* Includes other nonwhites

SOURCE: Prepared by Research Department of the National Urban League from unpublished data in U.S. Bureau of Labor Statistics.

Table 11

*Mean Scores for Performance of Household Tasks
as Reported by Lower-Class Males
by Race and Wives' Employment Status**

Household Tasks Performed	Black Males		White Males	
	(N = 28) With unemployed wives	(N = 81) With employed wives	(N = 77) With unemployed wives	(N = 45) With employed wives
1. Borrows money	3.6	3.0	3.2	2.7
2. Takes clothes to laundry	3.1	3.0	2.3	3.1
3. Disciplines children	2.8	2.9	1.4	1.8
4. Takes out garbage	2.8	2.9	2.4	2.1
5. Talks with landlord	2.7	2.0	2.4	2.1
6. Shops for groceries	2.5	2.2	2.7	2.4
7. Pays bills	2.4	1.3	2.1	1.8
8. Gets up at night with children	2.2	2.2	1.7	1.9
9. Prepares supper	1.4	1.4	1.2	1.5
10. Does laundry at home	1.2	1.2	1.2	1.4

* The scoring of the performance of household tasks (based upon the husbands' reports) was as follows: scores below two for "wife more often performed the task," scores 2.0–2.9 for "both spouses equally performed the task," and scores 3.0 and over for "husband more often performed the task."

SOURCE: Prepared by Research Department of the National Urban League from data in Joan Aldous, "Wives' Employment Status and Lower-Class Men as Husband-Fathers: Support for the Moynihan Thesis," *Journal of Marriage and the Family*, 31 (August 1969): 469–476. Esp. f.n. 28.

Table 12

Distribution of Mean Scores for Performance
of Ten Household Tasks as Reported by Lower-Class Males,
by Race and Wives' Employment Status

Household Tasks Performed by:	Black Males		White Males	
	With unemployed wives	*With employed wives*	*With unemployed wives*	*With employed wives*
Wife more often (Scores below 2)	2	3	4	5
Both equally (Scores 2.0–2.9)	6	5	5	3
Husband more often (Scores 3.0 and over)	2	2	1	2
Total number of tasks	10	10	10	10

SOURCE: Prepared by Research Department of the National Urban League from data in Joan Aldous, "Wives' Employment Status and Lower-Class Men as Husband-Fathers: Support for the Moynihan Thesis," *Journal of Marriage and the Family,* 31 (August 1969): 469–476. Esp. f.n. 28.

Table 13
Distribution of AFDC Families by Status of Father
*by Race, 1969**
(Numbers in thousands)

	Total	Black	White
Total AFDC families	1,593	737	836
Total percent	100	100	100
Father absent	81	90	73
Single	28	41	16
Deserted	16	19	12
Separated (legal/informal)	14	14	13
Other separated	4	4	5
Divorced	14	6	21
Widowed	5	6	5
Father present	19	11	24

* Excluding Puerto Rico and the Virgin Islands

SOURCE: Prepared by Research Department of the National Urban League from unpublished data from U.S. National Center for Social Statistics based on its 1969 AFDC national study.

Table 14
All Families and AFDC Families with Father Absent
by Reason for Absence, by Race, 1969*
(Numbers in thousands)

	AFDC Families			All Families	
	Total	*Black*	*White*	*Black*	*White*
Families with father absent	1,297	657	584	1,327	4,053
Total percent	100	100	100	100	100
Single	35	46	22	14	10
Deserted	19	21	17	—	—
Separated (legal/informal)	17	16	18	37	12
Other separated	5	4	7	6	8
Divorced	17	6	30	13	23
Widowed	7	7	6	31	48

* Excluding Puerto Rico and the Virgin Islands

SOURCE: Prepared by Research Department of the National Uurban League from data in U.S. Bureau of the Census, "Selected Characteristics of Persons and Families: March 1970," *Current Population Reports: Population Characteristics,* Series P–20, No. 204; and unpublished data from U.S. National Center for Social Statistics based on its 1969 AFDC national study.

Table 15

Suicide Rates for Selected Age Groups by Sex and Race, 1968
(Rates per 100,000 population)

Age	Male Black	White	Female Black	White
Total (all ages)	7.3	16.9	2.4	6.3
Under 1 year	—	—	—	—
5–9 years	—	0.0	—	—
15–19 years	4.7	8.3	2.2	2.2
20–24 years	13.1	15.0	4.4	4.8
25–29 years	16.0	16.3	4.5	7.0
30–34 years	16.1	18.3	4.8	8.1
35–39 years	12.0	22.0	4.7	10.6
45–49 years	12.1	27.0	3.8	13.1
55–59 years	13.3	35.8	3.1	12.3
65–69 years	12.8	35.6	3.5	8.3
75–79 years	15.0	42.5	4.7	7.2
85 years and over	5.5	56.8	2.8	4.9

SOURCE: Prepared by National Urban League Research Department from unpublished data in U.S. Department of Health, Education, and Welfare, Mortality Statistics Branch.

Table 16

Remarriages as Percent of All Marriages
for Black and White Brides, 1965, 1966, 1967, 1968[1]
(Numbers in thousands)

Race	1965	1966	1967	1968
Blacks[2]				
All marriages	127	109	112	122
Remarriages	24	20	21	22
Percent of all marriages	19	18	18	18
White				
All marriages	933	789	820	929
Remarriages	209	184	198	220
Percent of all marriages	22	24	24	24

[1] Data are for States that report a race and color breakdown. 39 States and the District of Columbia are marriage registration areas but some States do not have complete reporting by race. California, New York and Ohio do not report race or color at all.

[2] Includes other nonwhites.

SOURCE: Prepared by Research Department of the National Urban League from data in U.S. Public Health Service, National Center for Health Statistics, *Vital Statistics of the United States* for the years 1965, 1966, 1967 and 1968.

Table 17
Educational Level of Heads of Families
of Students Enrolled in College
by Race and Type of College, Fall 1970
(Percent distribution)

| Years of School Completed by Family Head | College Students | | | |
| | Race[1] | | Type of college[2] | |
	Black	White	Predominantly black	All colleges
Total family heads	100	100	100	100
Less than high school	54	24	57	27
High school graduate	21	36	24	29
Some college	12	15	9	17
4 years or more of college	14	26	11	27

[1] Students 16 to 34 years old enrolled in college as of October 1970 Current Population Survey of the Bureau of the Census. This excludes students who are themselves family heads, wives, and other married family members with spouse present; also persons in families in which head is a member of the armed forces.

[2] First-time, full-time students entering all colleges (combining 2 year and 4 year colleges and universities) and entering predominantly black colleges. Data are from a national survey conducted by the American Council on Education in fall 1970. Years of school completed for head of family refers to father's education only.

SOURCE: Prepared by Research Department of the National Urban League from data in U.S. Bureau of the Census, "School Enrollment: October 1970," *Current Population Reports: Population Characteristics*, Series P-20, No. 222; and American Council on Education, *National Norms for Entering College Freshman—Fall, 1970*.

Table 18

Parental Influence on College Attendance
by Family Background, Race and Sex of College Students
(Percent reporting parental influence)

Family Status*	Men		Women	
	Black	*White*	*Black*	*White*
Low status	75	71	90	81
High status	75	81	87	92

* Family status was determined by whether the father's occupation and both parents' educational level fell above or below the median according to the Duncan Socio-Economic Index.

SOURCE: Prepared by National Urban League Research Department from data in Edward E. Harris, "Personal and Parental Influences on College Attendance: Some Negro-White Differences," *Journal of Negro Education,* Vol. 39, No. 4, Fall 1970, Table 1, pp. 305–313.

Table 19

Occupational Aspirations of High School Students
by Status, Family Intactness, Race and Urbanism
(Percent with high occupational aspirations)[1]

Status[2] and Family Intactness	Urban		Rural	
	Black	*White*	*Black*	*White*
High status				
Complete	81	83	50	76
Broken	73	69	54	83
Low status				
Complete	59	51	52	45
Broken	63	51	56	44

[1] "High" occupational aspirations refer to choices among professional, technical and managerial occupations.

[2] Family status depended upon whether the fathers' education and occupation were both "high" or "low." The cutting points for "high" or "low" were not specified.

SOURCE: Prepared by National Urban League Research Department from data in Arthur Cosby, "Black-White Differences in Aspirations Among Deep South High School Students," *Journal of Negro Education,* Vol. 40, No. 1, Winter 1971, Table 2, pp. 17–21.

Table 20

*Actual and Estimated Drop-Out Rates One Year
After College Entrance by Students' Race, Sex
and Type of College, 1967*

Student Race and Type of College	Men		Women	
	Actual	*Estimated*	*Actual*	*Estimated*
Black students in black colleges	12.7	13.2	13.3	13.3
Black students in white colleges	7.4	14.3	20.3	23.9
White students in white colleges	12.4	12.3	13.9	13.7

SOURCE: Alan E. Bayer and Robert F. Boruch, "Black and White Freshmen Entering Four-Year Colleges, *Educational Record* (American Council on Education, Washington, D.C.), Fall 1969, Table 8, pp. 371–386.

Table 21

*Proportion of Black Families Headed by Women
by Area of Residence, 1940–1970*

Year	Total U.S.	Urban	Non-Urban*	
			Nonfarm	*Farm*
1970	28	28	29	19
1960	21	22	19	11
1950	18	19	18	9
1940	18	23	17	10

* Between 1940–1960, "non-urban" referred specifically to rural areas. But the 1970 figures for "non-urban" areas refer to "outside metropolitan" areas, which include areas that are neither rural nor metropolitan, in addition to rural areas. Thus the "sharp" rise in the proportion of families with women heads in non-urban areas between 1960 and 1970 is due to the Census Bureau's new classification of metropolitan-nonmetropolitan areas.

SOURCE: Prepared by Research Department of the National Urban League from data in U.S. Bureau of the Census: *Sixteenth Census of the United States: 1940 Population, Families; U.S. Census of Population: 1960, U.S. Summary, Detailed Characteristics;* "Selected Characteristics of Persons and Families: March 1970," *Current Population Reports: Population Characteristics,* Series P–20, No. 204. One-person "families" in the 1940 Census data were excluded in order to facilitate comparison with Census family composition data in subsequent years.

Table 22
*Proportion of All Families Headed by Women
by Race and Family Income, 1969*
(Percent families headed by women)

Family Income	Black	White	Percent Difference
Total	28	9	+19
Under $3,000	57	29	+28
$3,000–4,999	39	19	+20
5,000–6,999	26	13	+13
7,000–9,999	12	7	+5
10,000–14,999	7	4	+3
15,000 and over	6	3	+3

SOURCE: Prepared by Research Department of the National Urban League from data in U.S. Bureau of the Census, "Social and Economic Characteristics of the Population in Metropolitan and Nonmetropolitan Areas: 1970 and 1960," *Current Population Reports: Special Studies,* Series P–23, No. 37, Table 8.

Table 23
*Proportion of All Families Headed by Women
by Race, Area and Family Income, 1969*
(Percent families headed by women)

Family Income	Black families Metropolitan	Non-metropolitan	White families Metropolitan	Non-metropolitan
Total	28	28	10	8
Under $2,000	66	53	41	26
$2,000–3,999	61	33	28	17
4,000–5,999	34	22	19	11
6,000–7,999	21	10	14	7
8,000–9,999	12	5	8	5
10,000 and over	7	9	4	3

SOURCE: Prepared by Research Department of the National Urban League from data in U.S. Bureau of the Census, "Social and Economic Characteristics of the Population in Metropolitan and Nonmetropolitan Areas: 1970 and 1960," *Current Population Reports: Special Studies,* Series P–23, No. 37, Table 7.

NOTES

1. Frazier 1957 and 1966; Valentine 1968: 20–24.

   Although we feel that Frazier's analyses of low-income black families in urban areas tend to focus more on weaknesses than strengths, it is important to note that a reading of his actual works shows a more balanced treatment of urban black families than is commonly believed. We are particularly concerned about the exploitation of Frazier by contemporary social scientists who, despite the abundance of data presently available (which Frazier did not have), do not even bother to test and update his formulations. Instead, they popularize only his ideas that conform to their theses of pathology and matriarchy, and ignore his analyses which do not conform to their preconceptions, such as the "downfall of the matriarchate" and the primacy of the black male breadwinner.

2. Glazer and Moynihan 1965; Moynihan 1965 and 1966; Oscar Lewis 1966a.

3. Clark 1965; Grier and Cobbs 1968; Washington 1966.

4. Drake and Cayton 1962; Du Bois 1895; Johnson 1967; Billingsley 1968; Herzog 1966; Lewis 1955, 1966 and 1967; Valentine 1968.

5. Some of the authors who have drawn attention to black strengths are: Billingsley 1968; Herzog 1966; Ladner 1971; Lewis 1965; Keil 1966; J. Bernard 1966a; Coles 1964; Hannerz 1969; Liebow 1967; Phillips 1971; Proctor 1966 and 1971; Reissman 1966; Staples 1970 and 1971; Vontress 1971; Wasserman 1968; Willie 1970; Hobson 1971.

6. Parsons 1951; Parsons and Bales 1955.

7. Cohen and Hodges 1963; Bott 1957 and 1964; Feagin 1968.

8. U.S. Bureau of the Census, "Household and Family Characteristics: March 1970" Series P-20, No. 218, 1971, Tables 3 and 4.

9. Beck 1967; Drake and Cayton 1962; Frazier 1957, 1964, and 1966.

10. Herzog and Bernstein 1965; Deasy and Quinn 1962; Gallagher 1967; Olds 1968; Herzog, et al. 1971.

11. U.S. Bureau of the Census 1971b.

The illegitimacy rate among whites increased from 9.2 to 13.2 (per 1,000 unmarried women 15–44 years old) between 1960 and 1968, while the rate among blacks declined from 98.3 to 86.6 over the same period.

12. U.S. Bureau of the Census 1971c and 1971d show median income of black families to be 61 percent of median income of white families and poverty rate for blacks is more than 3 times that of whites. Bureau of Labor Statistics News, "The Employment Situation: June 1971," July 2, 1971 shows black unemployment rate as 9.4 compared to 5.2 for whites.

13. Tausky and Wilson 1971.

14. U.S. Office of Economic Opportunity 1970 and 1971.

15. U.S. Bureau of the Census 1971a

The recent Census-BLS report on blacks in 1970, which took account of the role of double earners, shows how illusory income parity can be. For that report revealed that, contrary to the impression conveyed by the earlier Census news release (1971a), the income gap between young black and white families where only the husband worked did not significantly close over the decade. See Bureau of the Census and Bureau of Labor Statistics 1971, Table 22.

16. Hannerz 1969b: 74–75.

17. Aldous 1969: 470–471.

18. U.S. Bureau of Labor Statistics 1971 presents data showing 1970 annual average unemployment rate for black adult men as 5.6 and for black adult women as 6.9.

19. U.S. Bureau of the Census 1970d; Harwood and Hodge 1971; Newman and Steffes 1971.

20. Kahl and Goering 1971: 309; Aldous 1969: 471, f.n. 19.

21. Aldous 1969; Coles 1964; Frazier 1957; Moynihan 1965; Rainwater 1966; Rodman 1963, 1964 and 1968; Schulz 1968 and 1969.

22. U.S. Bureau of the Census 1970c; See especially the impressive refutations of the myth of female dominance in Murray 1970 and

in Jacquelyn Jackson's soon-to-be published article, "Black Women in a Racist Society."

23. Otto 1962: 77–80.
24. Bott 1964; Coser 1964.
25. Moynihan 1965; Blood and Wolfe 1960.
26. Hyman and Reed 1969.
27. See following discussions of relative merits of self-reports versus observational techniques in studying decision-making: Olson 1969; Heer 1963; and Mack 1971.
28. Middleton and Putney 1960: 607.
29. Aldous 1969.
30. Although we have focused on the household task performance scores of lower-class families in Aldous' study, it should be noted that the findings in her study do suggest that black men with working wives in poor families participate less in decision-making and task performance in areas related to finances than do black men with nonworking wives.

   But our major focus is on the majority of husbands in low-income families. And we consider to be a major finding of this study that: the husbands in the majority of poor black families (which are mostly characterized by nonworking wives) participate in decision-making and the performance of household tasks to a greater extent than husbands in poor white families (whether they have working wives or not) or the minority of husbands in poor black families with working wives.
31. Parker and Kleiner 1966.
32. According to some investigations, the equalitarian family pattern also holds for elderly blacks as well. See Jackson 1971. Also see Ladner's distinction between "strength" and "dominance" in Ladner 1971: 35.
33. Merton 1957: 132.
34. Ross and Hill 1967: 168.
35. Herzog and Sudia 1970. See also comparison of fatherless families on welfare with fatherless families not on welfare in Bernard 1964.
36. See interesting discussion of "un-families" in Herzog and Sudia 1970: 82–84; Nye 1957.
37. Herzog and Sudia 1970.
38. See especially comparison of one and two parent lower-class black families in Wasserman 1968; Nye 1957.
39. Aug and Bright 1970.

40. *Ibid.:* 592.
41. See excellent longitudinal study of unwed mothers by N.Y.C. Community Council (1970).
42. Geismar and Ayres 1959; Geismar *et. al.* 1962.
43. Geismar and Gerhart 1968.
44. Moynihan 1965; Rainwater 1966; Schulz 1968; Rodman 1968.
45. Kephart and Monahan 1952.
46. U.S. Department of Health, Education, and Welfare 1970.
47. Merton 1957: 174.
48. Merton 1957: 411, f.n. 16.
49. Moynihan 1964; Aldous 1969; Rodman 1964 and 1968.
50. Johnsen and Leslie 1965: 357.
51. Rodman 1964; Frazier 1957 and 1966; Hare 1965. This equation of life styles with their indicators is referred to as the "fallacy of reification."
52. American Council on Education 1970. The statistics on Howard University's students were reported by Dr. James W. Bryant, Vice-President for Development and University Relations in April 1971 in a *Washington Post* article entitled "Howard University is Victimized by Elitist Reputation" (by Robert L. Asher).
53. U.S. Census Bureau 1970: "School Enrollment: October 1970."
54. Hindelang 1970.
55. Harris 1970.
56. Cosby 1971. Also see the Coleman Report, 1966, sections 3.13 and 3.26.
57. See Table 20.
58. Duncan and Duncan 1969; Proctor 1966.
59. Mays and Nicholson 1933; Clark 1965; Frazier 1964.
60. Frazier 1964 and 1966; Mays 1970. See especially Martin Luther King, Jr., *Stride Toward Freedom: The Montgomery Story,* New York: Harper, 1958.
61. Frazier 1964; Marx 1967.
62. Brink and Harris 1964: 103.
63. *Ibid.:* 221.
64. Proctor 1966; Mays and Nicholson 1933.
65. Garland 1971.
66. Cleage 1968; Mays 1970.

BIBLIOGRAPHY

Adams, Bert N. and James E. Butler. 1967
  "Occupational Status and Husband-Wife Social Participation," *Social Forces,* 45 (June): 501–507.

Aldous, Joan. 1969
  "Wives' Employment Status and Lower-Class Men as Husband-Fathers: Support for the Moynihan Thesis," *Journal of Marriage and the Family* 31 (August): 469–476.

Allport, Gorden W. 1958
  The Nature of Prejudice, Garden City, N.Y.: Doubleday. Esp. Chapter 28, "Religion and Prejudice."

American Council on Education, Office of Research. 1970
  "National Norms for Entering College Freshmen, Fall 1970, *ACE Research Reports,* 5 (December).

Aptheker, Herbert. 1971
  "Afro-American Superiority: A Neglected Theme in the Literature." In Goldstein, 1971, 165–179.

Aug, Robert G. and Thomas Bright. 1970
  "A Study of Wed and Unwed Motherhood in Adolescents and Young Adults," *Journal of the American Academy of Child Psychiatry,* 9 (October): 577–592.

Babchuk, Nicholas and Ralph V. Thompson. 1962
  "The Voluntary Association of Negroes," *American Sociological Review,* 27 (October): 647–655.

Bardolph, Richard. 1959
  The Negro Vanguard. New York: Holt, Rinehart and Winston.

Barbour, Floyd B. 1969

    The Black Power Revolt: A Collection of Essays. First Collier Books Edition.

Bayer, Alan E. and Robert F. Boruch. 1969

    "Black and White Freshmen Entering Four-Year Colleges," *Educational Record.* Washington, D.C. American Council on Education (Fall): 371–386.

Beck, James P. 1967

    "Limitations of One Social Class Index When Comparing Races With Respect to Indices of Health," *Social Forces,* 45 (June): 586–588.

Bell, Robert B. 1965a

    "The One-Parent Mother in the Negro Lower Class," Presented at Eastern Sociological Meetings, New York City.

——— 1965b

    "Lower Class Negro Mothers and their Children," *Integrated Education* 2 (December–January): 23–27.

Bernard, Jessie. 1966a

    Marriage and Family Among Negroes. Englewood Cliffs, N.J.: Prentice-Hall.

——— 1966b

    "Marital Stability and Patterns of Status Variables," *Journal of Marriage and the Family,* 28 (November): 421–439.

Bernard, Sydney E. 1964

    Fatherless Families: Their Economic and Social Adjustment, Waltham Massachusetts: Florence Heller Graduate School for Advanced Studies in Social Welfare, Brandeis University. A condensation of *The Economic and Social Adjustment of Low-Income Female-Headed Families,* Unpublished Ph.D. dissertation, 1964, Brandeis University.

Billingsley, Andrew. 1968

    Black Families in White America. Englewood Cliffs, N.J.: Prentice-Hall.

Blood, Robert O. Jr., and Donald M. Wolfe. 1960

    Husbands and Wives: The Dynamics of Married Living. Glencoe: Free Press. 1969

——— 1969

    "Negro-White Differences in Blue-Collar Marriages in a Northern Metropolis," *Social Forces,* 48 (September): 59–64.

Blumberg, Leonard and Robert R. Bell. 1959
    "Urban Migration and Kinship Ties," *Social Problems* 6 (Spring) 328–333.
Bond, Jean Carey and Pat Perry. 1970
    "Is the Black Male Castrated?" In Cade 1970, 113–118.
Bott, Elizabeth. 1957
    Family and Social Network, London: Tavistock.
———— 1964
    "Conjugal Roles and Social Network." In Coser 1964, 331–350.
Brink, William and Lewis Harris. 1964
    The Negro Revolution in America, New York: Simon and Schuster. Esp. Chapter 6, "The Role of the Negro Church."
———— 1967
    Black and White, New York: Simon and Schuster. Esp. Chapter 7, "The Negro Family."
Buttermann, Catherine M. 1968
    "The Multimarriage Family," *Social Casework,* 49 (April): 218–221.
Cade, Toni, ed. 1970
    The Black Woman: An Anthology. New York: Signet.
Clark, Kenneth. 1965
    Dark Ghetto, New York: Harper and Row.
Cleage, Jr., Albert B. 1968
    The Black Messiah, New York: Sheed and Ward.
Cohen, Albert K. and Harold M. Hodges, Jr. 1963
    "Characteristics of the Lower-Blue-Collar Class," *Social Problems,* (Spring): 303–334.
Coles, Robert. 1964
    Children of Crisis, New York: Little, Brown.
Comer, J. P. 1970
    "The Black Family: An Adaptive Perspective," New Haven: Child Study Center, Yale University. Mimeo.
Community Council of Greater New York, Research Department. 1970
    The Six-Year Experience of Unwed Mothers as Parents: A Continuing Study of These Mothers and Their Children. New York City.
Cosby, Arthur. 1971
    "Black-White Differences in Aspirations Among Deep South High School Students," *Journal of Negro Education,* 40 (Winter): 17–21.

Coser, Rose L., ed. 1964
 The Family: Its Structure and Functions, New York: St. Martin's Press.

Cruse, Harold. 1967
 The Crisis of the Negro Intellectual. New York: William Morrow and Company.

Curtis, Jr., Russell L. and Louis A. Zurcher, Jr. 1971
 "Voluntary Associations and the Social Integration of the Poor," *Social Problems,* 18 (Winter): 339–357.

Davis, Angela. 1971
 "Rhetoric Vs. Reality," *Ebony* 26 (July): 115.120. Also "The Radicalization of Angela Davis," in the same issue.

Deasy, Leila Calhoun and Olive Westbrooke Quinn. 1962
 "The Urban Negro and Adoption of Children," *Child Welfare,* Journal of the Child Welfare League of America, Inc.

Dubois, W. E. B. 1967
 The Philadelphia Negro. New York: Schoken (First edition 1895)

Dentler, Robert A. and Mary Ellen Warshaver. 1968
 Big City Dropouts and Illiterates. New York: Frederick Praeger.

Dotson, Floyd. 1951
 "Patterns of Voluntary Association Among Urban Working Class Families," *American Sociological Review.*

Drake, St. Clair and Horace R. Clayton. 1962
 Black Metropolis. New York: Harper Torchbooks, 1962 (First edition 1945, Harcourt, Brace)

Duncan, Otis D. and Beverly Duncan. 1969
 "Family Stability and Occupational Success," *Social Problems* 16 (Winter): 273–285.

Durkheim, Emile. 1951
 Suicide, Translated by John A. Spaulding and George Simpson. Glencoe: The Free Press.

Epps, Edgar G., Irwin Katz and Leland J. Axelson. 1964
 "Intellectual Performance of Negro Students," *Social Problems,* 2 (Spring).

Fancher, Betsy. 1971
 "Black Colleges: The Struggle to Survive Is Even More Desperate Now," *South Today* 2 (June): 4–9.

Fanon, Frantz. 1963
 Black Skins, White Masks. New York: Grove Press.

Farley, Reynolds and Albert I. Hermalin. 1971
"Family Stability: A Comparison of Trends Between Blacks and Whites," *American Sociological Review* 36 (February): 1–17.

Feagin, Joe. 1968
"The Kinship Ties of Negro Urbanites," *Social Science Quarterly*, 49 (December): 660–665.

Frazier, E. Franklin. 1957a
Black Bourgeoisie, New York: The Free Press.

———— 1957b
The Negro in the United States, New York: The MacMillan Company.

———— 1964
The Negro Church in America. New York: Schocken Books.

———— 1966
The Negro Family in the United States. Chicago: University of Chicago Press. (First edition 1939)

Fried, Marc and Peggy Gleicher. 1961
"Some Sources of Residential Satisfaction in an Urban Slum," *Journal of the American Institute of Planners* 27 (November). Reprinted in Harold Proshansky, et. al, eds. *Environmental Psychology*. New York: Holt, Rinehart and Winston, 1970.

Gallagher, Ursula M. 1967
"Adoption, Current Trends," *Welfare in Review*, U.S. Department of Health, Education, and Welfare, 5 (February).

Gans, Herbert J. 1962
The Urban Villagers, New York: The Free Press.

Garland, Phyl. 1971
"The Unorthodox Ministry of Leon H. Sullivan," *Ebony*, 26 (May): 112–120.

Geismar, Ludwig L. and Beverly Ayres. 1959
"A Method for Evaluating the Social Functioning of Families Under Treatment," *Social Work*, 4 (January): 102–108.

Geismar, Ludwig and Ursula Gerhart. 1968
"Social Class, Ethnicity and Family Functioning: Exploring Some Issues Raised by the Moynihan Report," *Journal of Marriage and the Family*, 30 (August): 480–487.

Geismar, Ludwig, *et. al.* 1962
"Measuring Family Disorganization," *Marriages and Family Living*, 24 (February): 51–56.

Ginzberg, Eli and Associates. 1967

The Middle-Class Negro in the White Man's World, New York: Columbia University Press.

Gist, Noel P. and William S. Bennett, Jr. 1963

"Aspirations of Negro and White Students" *Social Forces*, 42 (October): 40–48.

Glazer, Nathan and Daniel P. Moynihan. 1965

Beyond the Melting Pot. Cambridge, Mass.: MIT Press.

Glick, Paul and Arthur Norton. 1971

"Frequency, Duration and Probability of Marriage and Divorce," *Journal of Marriage and the Family*, 33 (May).

Goldstein, Bernard. 1967

Low Income Youth in Urban Areas: A Critical Review of the Literature, New York: Holt, Rinehart and Winston.

Goldstein, Rhoda L., ed. 1971

Black Life and Culture in the United States, New York: Thomas Y. Crowell.

Grier, William H. and Price M. Cobbs. 1968

Black Rage, New York: Basic Books.

——— 1971

The Jesus Bag, New York: McGraw-Hill.

Hannerz, Ulf. 1969a

"The Roots of Black Manhood," *Transaction* (October): 12–21.

——— 1969b

Soulside: Inquiries into Ghetto Culture and Community, New York: Columbia University Press.

Hare, Nathan. 1965

Black Anglo-Saxons, New York: Marzone and Munsell.

Harwood, Edwin and Claire Hodge. 1971

"Jobs and the Negro Family," *Public Interest* 23 (Spring): 125–131.

Harris, Edward E. 1970

"Personal and Parental Influences in College Attendance: Some Negro-White Differences," *Journal of Negro Education*, 39 (Fall): 305–313.

Hartnagel, Timothy F. 1970

"Father Absence and Self Conception Among Lower Class White and Negro Boys," *Social Problems*, 18 (Fall): 152–163.

Heer, David M. 1963

"The Measurement and Bases of Family Power," *Marriage and Family Living*, 251.

Henry, A. F. and J. F. Short. 1964
    Homicide and Suicide, New York: Free Press.
Herskovits, Melville. 1958
    The Myth of the Negro Past, Boston: Beacon Press.
Herzog, Elizabeth. 1966
    "Is There a 'Breakdown' of the Negro Family?" *Social Work*
    (January). Reprinted in Rainwater and Yancey 1967.
——— 1968
    "About the Poor: Some Facts and Some Fictions," Washing-
    ton: Government Printing Office.
Herzog, Elizabeth and Rose Bernstein. 1965
    "Why So Few Negro Adoptions?" *Children,* U.S. Department
    of Health, Education and Welfare, January–February.
Herzog, Elizabeth and Hylan Lewis. 1970
    "Children in Poor Families: Myths and Realities," *American
    Journal of Orthopsychiatry,* 40, 3 (April): 375–387.
Herzog, Elizabeth and Cecelia E. Sudia. 1967
    "Family Structure and Composition," *Race, Research and Rea-
    son: Social Work Perspective.* New York: National Association of
    Social Workers, 145–164.
——— 1970
    Boys in Fatherless Families. Washington, D.C., U.S. Depart-
    ment of Health, Education and Welfare, Office of Child Develop-
    ment, Children's Bureau. To be published in *Review of Child
    Development Research,* Vol. 3.
Herzog, Elizabeth, et. al. 1971
    Families for Black Children: The Search for Adoptive Parents.
    A report of the Division of Research and Evaluation, Children's
    Bureau, Office of Child Development and the Social Research
    Group, The George Washington University.
Hindelang, Michael James. 1970
    "Educational and Occupational Aspirations Among Working
    Class Negro, Mexican-American and White Elementary School
    Children," *Journal of Negro Education,* 39 (Fall): 351–353.
Hobson, Sheila Smith. 1971
    "The Black Family—Together in Every Sense," *Tuesday At
    Home Magazine,* (Sunday newspaper supplement) (April): 12–34.
Holloway and Berreman. 1959
    "The Educational and Occupational Plans for Negro and

White Elementary School Children," *Pacific Sociological Review,* 7: 56–60.

Hyman, Herbert H. 1953

"The Value Systems of Different Classes," In Reinhard Bendix and Seymour M. Lipset, *Class, Status and Power.* Glencoe: The Free Press, 426–442.

Hyman, Herbert H. and John Shelton Reed. 1969

"Black Matriarchy Reconsidered: Evidence from Secondary Analysis of Sample Surveys," *Public Opinion Quarterly,* 33 (Fall): 346–354.

Jackson, Jacquelyn. 1971

"Marital Life Among Aging Blacks," Department of Psychiatry, Duke University Medical Center, Durham, North Carolina, Mimeo.

Jaffe, A. J. and Walter Adams. 1964

"College Education for U.S. Youth: The Attitudes of Parents and Children," *American Journal of Economics and Sociology,* 3 (July): 269–284.

Jaffe, A. J., Walter Adams and Sandra G. Meyers. 1968

Negro Higher Education in the 1960's. New York: Frederick Praeger.

Johnsen, Kathryn P. and Gerald R. Leslie. 1965

"Methodological Notes in Research in Child-Rearing and Social Class," *Merrill-Palmer Quarterly,* 11 (October): 345–358.

Johnson, Charles S. 1967

Growing Up in the Black Belt, Washington, D.C.

Kahl, Joseph. 1953

"Educational and Occupational Aspirations of 'Common Man' Boys," *Harvard Educational Review,* 23 (Summer): 168–203.

Kahl, Joseph A. and John M. Goering. 1971

"Stable Workers, Black and White," *Social Problems* (Winter): 306–318.

Katz, Maude White. 1970

"End Racism in Education: A Concerned Parent Speaks," In Cade 1970, 124–131.

Keil, Charles. 1966

Urban Blues, Chicago: University of Chicago.

Killian, Lewis M. and Charles M. Grigg. 1964

"Negro Perceptions of Organizational Effectiveness," *Social Problems,* 11 (Spring): 380–388..

King, Martin Luther, Jr. 1958
Stride Toward Freedom: The Montgomery Story, New York: Harper.

Komarovsky, Mira. 1964
Blue Collar Marriage, New York: Random House.

Kephart, William M., and Thomas P. Monahan. 1952
"Desertion and Divorce in Philadelphia," *American Sociological Review,* 17 (October): 719–727.

Krauss, Irving. 1964
"Sources of Educational Aspirations Among Working Class Youth," *American Sociological Review,* 29 (December): 867–879.

Ladner, Joyce A. 1971
Tomorrow's Tomorrow: The Black Woman. Garden City, N.Y.: Doubleday.

Lenski, Gerhard. 1961
The Religious Factor. Garden City, N.Y.: Doubleday.

Leslie, Gerald R. and Kathryn P. Johnsen. 1963
"Changed Perceptions of the Maternal Role," *American Sociological Review* 28 (December): 919–928.

Lewis, Hylan. 1955
Blackways of Kent. Chapel Hill: University of North Carolina Press.

―――― 1965
"The Family: Resources for Change," Agenda Paper No. 5, Planning Session, White House Conference "To Fulfill These Rights," November, 1965. Reprinted in Rainwater and Yancey, 1967.

―――― 1966
"Family Life Among an Urban Low-Income Population Under a Federally Guaranteed Minimum Income Plan. 1991–1996." A draft prepared for discussion at Conference on Guaranteed Minimum Income, University of Chicago, January 14–15, 1966.

―――― 1967
Culture, Class and Poverty, Washington Health and Welfare Council of the National Capital Area, Project CROSS-TELL. Adapted from three papers presented at conferences held between 1961–1964.

Lewis, Oscar. 1961
The Children of Sanchez. New York: Random House.

———— 1966a
"The Culture of Poverty," *Scientific American*, 215: 19–25.

———— 1966b
Lavida: A Puerto Rican Family in the Culture of Poverty—San Juan and New York. New York: Random House.

Liebow, Elliot. 1967
Tally's Corner: A Study of Negro Streetcorner Men. Boston: Little, Brown.

Mack, Delores E. 1971
"Where the Black-Matriarchy Theorists Went Wrong," *Psychology Today*, 4 (January): 24, 86–88.

Marx, Gary T. 1967a
"Religion: Opiate or Inspiration of Civil Rights Militancy Among Negroes?" *American Sociological Review*, 32 (February): 64–72.

———— 1967b
Protest and Prejudice. New York: Harper and Row.

Mays, Benjamin E. 1970
Born to Rebel: New York: Scribner.

Mays, Benjamin E. and Joseph W. Nicholson. 1933
The Negro's Church. New York: Institute of Social and Religious Research.

Merton, Robert K. 1957
Social Theory and Social Structure, Glencoe: The Free Press.

Middleton, Russell and Shell Putney. 1960
"Dominance in the Family: Role and Class Differences," *American Journal of Sociology*, 65 (May): 605–609.

Moynihan, Daniel P. 1965
The Negro Family: The Call For National Action. Washington U.S. Department of Labor. Reprinted in Rainwater and Yancey 1967.

———— 1966
"Employment, Income and Ordeal of the Negro Family," in Parsons and Clark 1966.

———— 1967
"The President and the Negro: The Moment Lost," *Commentary* 43:31–45.

Murray, Pauli. 1970
"The Liberation of Black Women," in Mary Lou Thompson (ed.) *Voices of the New Feminism*. Boston: Beacon Press, 87–102.

National Urban League, Research Department. 1970
"The Black Colleges: Their Characteristics and Trends."
Mimeo.

Newman, Dorothy K. and Robert B. Steffes. 1971
"Occupational Attainment of Ethnic Groups and Women in
15 Industries," Washington, D.C., National Urban League Research Department. A report prepared for the U.S. Equal Opportunity Commission (EEOC).

Nye, F. Ivan. 1957
"Child Adjustment in Broken and in Unhappy Homes," *Marriage and Family Living* 19 (November): 356–361.

Olds, Charles B. 1968
"Results of Survey of Interracial Adoption in the United
States in 1968," *Opportunity: A Program to Broaden Adoption
Opportunities for Children of Negro Ancestry,* Portland, Oregon,
September.

Olsen, Marvin. 1970
"Social and Political Participation of Blacks," *American Sociological Review* 35 (August): 632–697.

Olson, David H. 1969
"The Measurement of Family Power by Self-Report and Behavioral Methods," *Journal of Marriage and the Family,* 31 (August): 545–550.

Otto, Herbert A. 1962
"What Is a Strong Family?" *Marriage and Family Living* 24
(February): 72–80.

Parker, Seymour and Robert J. Kleiner. 1966
"Characteristics of Negro Mothers in Single-Headed Households," *Journal of Marriage and the Family,* 28 (November): 507–513.

——— 1969
"Social and Psychological Dimensions of the Family Role Performance of the Negro Male," *Journal of Marriage and the Family,* 31 (August): 500–506.

Parsons, Talcott. 1951
The Social System, New York: The Free Press.

Parsons, Talcott and Robert F. Bales. 1955
Family Socialization and Interaction Process. New York: The
Free Press.

Parsons, Talcott and Kenneth B. Clark, eds. 1966
The Negro American. The Daedalus Library, Vol. 7, New York: Houghton Mifflin.

Passow, A. Harry, ed. 1963
Education in Depressed Areas, New York: Bureau of Publications, Teachers College, Columbia University.

Phillips, Jr., W. M. 1971
"Survival Techniques of Black Americans." In Goldstein 1971, 153–164.

Poinsett, Alex. 1971
"The Dilemma of the Black Policemen," *Ebony,* 26 (May): 122–131.

Proctor, Samuel D. 1966
The Young Negro in America: 1960–1980. New York: Association Press.

———— 1971
"Survival Techniques and the Black Middle Class." In Goldstein 1971, 280–294.

Rainwater, Lee. 1960
And the Poor Get Children, Chicago: Quadrangle Books.

———— 1966
"Crucible of Identity: The Negro Lower Class Family," In Parsons and Clark 1966.

Rainwater, Lee and William L. Yancey. 1967
The Moynihan Report and the Politics of Controversy. Cambridge: M.I.T. Press.

Record, Wilson. 1953
"Role of Negro Intellectuals," *Crisis,* 60 (June–July).

Reissman, Frank. 1966
"In Defense of the Negro Family," *Dissent* (March–April): 141–155.

Rodman, Hyman. 1963
"The Lower-Class Value Stretch," *Social Forces* 42 (December): 205–215.

———— 1964
"Middle-Class Conceptions About Lower-Class Families." In Shostak and Gomberg 1964.

———— 1968
"Family and Social Pathology in the Ghetto." *Science,* 161 (August): 756–761.

Rosen, Lawrence. 1969
    "Matriarchy and Lower Class Negro Male Delinquency," *Social Problems,* 17 (Fall): 175–189.

Ross, Arthur M. and Herbert Hill, eds. 1967
    Employment, Race and Poverty. New York: Harcourt, Brace and World.

Schulz, David. 1968
    "Variations in the Father Role in Complete Families of the Negro Lower Class," *Social Science Quarterly,* 49 (December): 651–659.

—— 1969
    Coming Up Black: Patterns of Ghetto Socialization. Englewood Cliffs, N.J.: Prentice-Hall.

Shostak, Arthur B., and William Gomberg, eds. 1964
    Blue-Collar World: Studies of the American Worker. Englewood Cliffs, N.J.: Prentice-Hall.

Simpson, R. L. 1962
    "Parental Influence, Anticipatory Socialization and Social Mobility," *American Sociological Review,* 27 (August): 517–522.

Staples, Robert. 1970
    "The Myth of the Black Matriarchy," *The Black Scholar,* (February): 9–16.

—— 1971
    "The Myth of the Impotent Black Male," *The Black Scholar* 2 (June): 2–9.

—— 1971
    The Black Family: Essays and Studies. Belmont, California: Wadsworth.

Stein, Robert L. 1970
    "The Economic Status of Families Headed by Women," *Monthly Labor Review,* 93 (December): 3–10.

Stephenson, R. 1957
    "Mobility Orientation of 1000 Ninth Graders," *American Sociological Review* 22 (April): 204–212.

Stouffer, Samuel A. 1966
    Communism, Conformity and Civil Liberties. New York: Science Editions Paperback. (First edition 1955, Doubleday)

Strodtbeck, F. L. 1951
    "Husband-Wife Interaction over Revealed Differences," *American Sociological Review,* 16 (August): 468–473.

Tausky, Curt and William J. Wilson. 1971
    "Work Attachment Among Black Men," *Phylon* 32 (Spring): 23–30.
Thompson, Daniel C. 1963
    The Negro Leadership Class. Englewood Cliffs, N.J.: Prentice-Hall.
Udry, J. Richard. 1966
    "Marital Instability by Race, Sex, Education and Occupation Using 1960 Census Data," *American Journal of Sociology* 72 (September): 203–209.
U.S. Bureau of the Census. 1958
    "Religion Reported by the Civilian Population of the U.S.: March 1957," *Current Population Reports, Population Characteristics,* Series P-20, No. 79, February 2.
—— 1970a
    "Selected Characteristics of Persons and Families, March 1970," *Current Population Reports, Population Characteristics,* Series P-20, No. 204, July 13.
—— 1970b
    "Probabilities of Marriage, Divorce and Remarriage," *Current Population Reports, Special Studies,* Series P-23, No. 32, July 29.
—— 1970c
    "Educational Attainment: March 1970," *Current Population Reports, Population Characteristics,* Series P-20, No. 207, November 30, Table 1.
—— 1970d
    "Income in 1969 of Families and Persons in the United States," *Current Population Reports, Consumer Income,* Series P-60, No. 75, December 14.
—— 1971a
    "Differences Between Incomes of White and Negro Husband-Wife Families are Relatively Small Outside the South," *U.S. Department of Commerce News,* February 18.
—— 1971b
    "Fertility Indicators: 1970," *Current Population Reports, Special Studies,* Series P-23, No. 36, April 16.
—— 1971c
    "Poverty Increases by 1.2 Million in 1970," *Current Population Reports, Consumer Income,* Series P-60, No. 77, May 7.
—— 1971d

"Median Family Income Up in 1970," *Current Population Reports, Consumer Income,* Series P-60, No. 78, May 20.

U.S. Bureau of the Census and Bureau of Labor Statistics. 1970
"The Social and Economic Status of Negroes in the United States, 1969," *Current Population Reports, Special Studies,* Series P-23, No. 29 and BLS Report No. 375.

—— 1971
"The Social and Economic Status of Negroes in the United States, 1970," *Current Population Reports, Special Studies,* Series P-23, No. 38 and BLS Report No. 394.

U.S. Bureau of Labor Statistics. 1971
Employment and Earnings, 17, 8 (February).

U.S. Department of Health, Education and Welfare. 1964
America's Children and Youth in Institutions, 1950–1960–1964 Children's Bureau.

—— 1968
Vital Statistics of the U.S., 1968, Vol. 1—Natality, National Center for Health Statistics.

—— 1969
Adoptions in 1969; Supplement to Child Welfare Statistics 1969, National Center for Social Statistics.

—— 1970
"Preliminary Report on Findings—1969 AFDC Study," National Center for Social Statistics, Social and Rehabilitation Service, March.

U.S. Office of Economic Opportunity. 1970
"Preliminary Results of the New Jersey Work Incentive Experiments," OEO Pamphlet, February 18.

—— 1971
"Further Preliminary Results: The New Jersey Graduated Work Incentive Experiment." OEO Pamphlet, May.

Valentine, Charles A. 1968
Culture and Poverty: Critique and Counter-Proposals. Chicago: The University of Chicago Press.

Vontress, Clemmont E. 1971
"The Black Male Personality," *The Black Scholar.* 2 (June): 10–16.

Washington, Jr., Joseph R. 1966
Black Religion. Boston: Beacon Press.

Wasserman, Herbert L. 1968
   *Father-Absent and Father-Present Lower Class Negro Families:
   A Comparative Study of Family Functioning.* Unpublished Ph.D.
   dissertation, Florence Heller Graduate School for Advanced Studies
   in Social Welfare, Brandeis University.
Watts, Harold W. 1969
   "Graduated Work Incentives: Progress Toward an Experiment
   in Negative Taxation," Institute for Research on Poverty, Madi-
   son: The University of Wisconsin.
Williams, Helen. 1970
   "The Black Social Workers' Dilemma," in Cade 1970, 170–179.
Willie, Charles V. 1970
   The Family Life of Black People. Columbus, Ohio: Charles E.
   Merrill.
Wright, Charles R. and Herbert H. Hyman. 1958
   "Voluntary Association Memberships of American Adults: Evi-
   dence from National Sample Surveys," *American Sociological Re-
   view* 23 (June): 284–294.
Young, Jr., Whitney M. 1969
   Beyond Racism: Building An Open Society. New York:
   McGraw-Hill.